Leadership Values

AN INTROSPECTION

Copyright © 2019 by Gary F. Appleby

All rights reserved.

ISBN (paperback): 978-1-7329972-0-2

ISBN: (ebook): 978-1-7329972-1-9

No part of this publication may be reproduced, distributed, or transmitted in any form or by any means, including photocopying, recording, or other electronic or mechanical methods, without the prior written permission of the publisher, except in the case of brief quotations embodied in critical reviews and certain other noncommercial uses permitted by copyright law.

Cover and Interior Design by TeaBerryCreative.com

Leadership Values

AN INTROSPECTION

*A Philadelphia Fire Chief's
Forty-Year Journey
to Understanding and Practicing
Authentic Leadership*

Gary F. Appleby

THIS WORK IS DEDICATED TO—

Every leader who has ever fallen down, screwed up, or disappointed anyone–and then had the courage to make it right.

Contents

PROLOGUE   RAY ix
INTRODUCTION xiv

CHAPTER 1   INTEGRITY 1
             The Devil's Recruitment Team 9
CHAPTER 2   VISION 18
             A Special Place 30
CHAPTER 3   DECISIVENESS 43
             Gut Feeling 49
CHAPTER 4   SELF-DISCIPLINE 56
             The Weasel 60
CHAPTER 5   ACCOUNTABILITY 69
             The Captain Was A Con Man 73
CHAPTER 6   OPTIMISM 80
             "There Won't Even Be Enough Left of Us to Bury" 84
CHAPTER 7   COURAGE 93
             The Aroma Of Marinara 100
CHAPTER 8   HONESTY 108
             Three Little Buttons 113
CHAPTER 9   TRUSTWORTHINESS 117
             Deciding Who Lives—And Who Dies 123

LEADERSHIP VALUES

CHAPTER 10	PRIDE	131
	Ace	135
CHAPTER 11	COMPASSION	146
	Underneath Day	151
CHAPTER 12	LOYALTY	159
	A Brick to the Forehead and Other Leadership Advice	165
CHAPTER 13	HUMILITY	179
	Too Big For My Britches	185
CHAPTER 14	ENLIGHTENMENT	197
	The Firebombing	205
EPILOGUE		213

Prologue

THIS IS A TRUE STORY. Firefighters reading this may shudder at the safety violations, but this event occurred when bunker gear and protective hoods were not yet commonplace and the Fire Service lacked today's strict mandates for officer and crew integrity and accountability.

RAY

My thoughts were coming rapidly. At first, I thought, *This could be a problem.* Only a few seconds later, the reality hit me harder, *Hey, I'm in real trouble here.* Not long afterward, the dire urgency of the situation gripped my entire body as I realized, *Oh God, I'm going to die here.*

I see it clearly now: that cool, summer night in 1968, when another firefighter and I advanced a hoseline deep into the basement of an old, large, burning West Philly church—I was *supposed* to die. My creator had a plan and June 27th was going to be my final night on earth; twenty-two years was to be all I got. That "plan" centered on a sudden flashover in the basement of a Methodist church that would leave me burned to death. Naturally, the standard firefighter memorials attesting that my life as a Philadelphia Firefighter had some value would follow.

However, my companion on the 1½" hoseline, who was frantically directing the nozzle back and forth on a vast overhead sea of raging, expanding-by-the-minute fire had a different plan.

I hardly knew the other firefighter; his name was Ray. He was quiet and unassuming, and nearing retirement. Ray was assigned to Engine 65, just down Haverford Avenue, about a half-mile east of my beloved Ladder Company 24. We always said hello to each other on the fireground or other locations, but I never had a lengthy conversation with him. He just seemed to be one of those low-key, utterly dependable, "background people" who were thankfully sprinkled in every firehouse, on every platoon, throughout the city. He had zero "flash"; you just knew that he was fully content to be a team player.

As Ray and I advanced the hoseline down the basement stairs in thick black smoke and crawled across a large open area to engage the fire, everything seemed routine. We were about 150 feet in from the 54th Street side entrance; it was scary and heart-pounding, but not unlike anything I'd encountered

AN INTROSPECTION

before. I had been in a few similar situations in my two years as a firefighter.

Then, in what seemed like an instant, all the thick black smoke above us began to ignite. I first noticed the startling, almost instantaneous illumination. *How could this be? Did somebody turn the basement lights on?* Within seconds, it was so bright that I could see everything clearly through my air-mask: the square, red and white floor tiles; the stacked storage; even Ray. However, the "illumination" was simply a deadly prelude to the fire's full flashover effect. The ignition started at the far wall, as layers of brightly colored flames burst forth and swirled violently toward and then over us. *Oh God*, I thought to myself, *this could be a problem.*

Ray turned back to me and grabbed my running coat collar with his gloved hand. He pulled me closer and yelled though his mask, "We gotta crawl out of here, Kid. I'll follow the hoseline. Hang on to my leg tight—don't let go!" As soon as we started retreating on our bellies toward the old, wooden steps, my brain screamed, *Hey, I'm in real trouble here.*

As we crawled toward the stairs that had led us down into this furnace-like Hell, I felt like I was being baked. Every part of my body was intensely hot, especially my unprotected neck. Once we got to the base of the stairs, Ray yelled back, "Don't lose me; we gotta go fast!" At that point, we actually ascended through the irregular edges of the swirling flame front hugging the ceiling. As we rose up the stairs, my grip slipped from Ray's calf down to his ankle.

When we emerged onto the main floor, Ray paused, reached back, and pulled me closer, while placing my steaming glove hand back on his right calf. It was pitch black and incredibly hot. I knew that if we veered off of that hoseline, we were going to die. We didn't crawl as quickly as we had before; I guess Ray was running out of gas, or adrenalin, or both.

Parts of the old wood flooring were beginning to sag and through small cracks in the seventy-year old planking, I could see the flames churning below us. Worse yet, I was now being baked on my front side. At some point, I heard Ray's low-air warning activate. That was the moment that reality set in: *Oh, God, I'm going to die here!*

But not if Ray could help it. He kept methodically extending both his hands forward grasping the hoseline and crawling; we probably only gained about two feet at a time. Ray guided me along with each heave and periodically reached back to touch me. By that point, he had stopped talking.

When we reached the large, swinging vestibule doors, we found they'd been left partially open. Tommy Rosini, a firefighter from Ladder 24, had propped a chair against one door. He knew that we were still in the basement and if we had any chance of escape, we would have to return by retracing the hoseline through those heavy oak doors. Once into the

AN INTROSPECTION

vestibule, Ray rose to one knee and reached back for me. In one final herculean thrust of forward momentum, he launched the two of us forward. We both tumbled through the side entrance doors onto the large, top concrete step. Witnesses said our clothing and our hair were smoldering.

The first words I heard were from a nearby firefighter screaming, "They're alive!" Just two simple words, but they verified my nearness to death. My first visual memory while laying on that step was Ladder 24's plastic cab dome-light melting from the extreme radiant heat; the red plastic was running down the fire engine windshield onto the cab. I heard third-alarm units acknowledging their responses on radio as the fire roared spectacularly from every window in the church.

Believe it or not, neither of us was hospitalized. And Ray never received any commendation for saving me. But maybe the hardest thing of all to believe is that Ray and I never talked about that night's experience. Never.

Introduction

SO, WHAT DOES THE CHURCH FIRE STORY HAVE TO DO WITH THIS BOOK? And leadership values? For me, everything. That harrowing, near-death event led to two remarkable epiphanies that changed my life and stay within me to this very day.

First, it crystallized exactly what it meant to be a firefighter. After the fire, I spent weeks thinking about the lessons Ray's behavior held for me. Why didn't he leave me and focus on saving himself? How was I to think of him after that? What term would, or could, adequately describe his relevance in my life? Would I refer to him as a "co-worker" or a "fellow employee"? In the beginning, as I searched for understanding, any words that I came up with never came close to matching his actions.

The answer came to me gradually, like someone opening Venetian blinds to slowly allow the sunshine in. My formal Fire School training had included extensive discussions on the concept and value of "Fire Service Brotherhood." These lectures on brotherhood were almost as numerous as lessons about hoselines, ladders, strategies, and tactics.

AN INTROSPECTION

This brotherhood that the instructors preached seemed to be an important foundation piece of the Philadelphia Fire Department.

I realized that *was* it; the explanation for Ray's actions can be found in this notion of brotherhood. People may not risk their life for a co-worker or a fellow-employee; but, risk it for a brother? Yes; *that's* a completely different matter. People will do extraordinary things for family members.

With that, I finally understood what had happened in that burning basement; Ray saw me as his brother. We would get out together, or we would die together. Either way, we were going to experience the outcome *together*.

From that moment forward, I kept the notion of brotherhood in my frontal lobe during my entire career. It provided me with clarity and compelled me to try to be a better "family member." Wherever I served—line or staff, commercial or residential, uptown or South Philly—I felt truly honored and blessed to be a firefighter. I was part of the American Fire Service; therefore, I was part of *The Brotherhood*. I had found something in my life that was good, pure, meaningful, and devoid of hype and bullshit. I held on to it tightly—for over forty years.

My second realization was that many people, like Ray, have deep-rooted values that cause them to consistently act *automatically* in a certain positive (or negative) fashion. There are specific circumstances when many of us require additional time to think through, evaluate, or deliberate on the personal consequences of actions we are considering.

Yet these principled individuals just rely on their internal moral compass and move quickly toward positive action.

The nearly instantaneous decisions that these people routinely make on the toughest of issues is rooted in their goodness. They are incapable of living their life in any other way because their internal compass is steadfastly fixed on living their personal values.

When the danger arose that night in the church basement, Ray's personal value system automatically kicked in. He didn't have to evaluate how much exit time he would lose with me holding onto his leg. He didn't have to deliberate on the positives and negatives of looking out for me. He didn't have to think through anything. His immediate reaction to the threat was simply based on who he was; his personal values left him no real choice.

THE FOURTEEN LEADERSHIP VALUES

Following the fire, I knew that I needed to learn more about human values. So, as a young firefighter in West Philly's Eleventh Battalion, I began to quietly observe and evaluate the behavior of every leader with whom I came in contact. I wanted to learn why some of my leaders were wonderful, while others made me question the validity of the entire civil service promotional system.

My learning methodology was not rooted so much in listening to their words, for they all had different levels of oratory skills. Rather, I focused on:

AN INTROSPECTION

- What did the leader believe in?
- What factors guided the leader's decisions?
- What was the leader willing to fight for?

I soon realized that values are an important reason why people act the way they do. It became clear to me that our experiences and beliefs form the core of our individual value system and that many of our strongest values are passed to us through our families, friends, organizations, and associations.

After some time, distinct patterns began to emerge from observations I made both in the fire station and on emergency scenes. Although clearly unscientific, my "research" indicated that the leaders who I respected the most had much in common. In time, I came to understand that people with positive values, especially leaders, can be loosely grouped together based on a commonality that revolves primarily around their consistent, exemplary, personal behavior, and how they treat others.

That is the basis for this book: relaying to you, in specific terms, what I saw, what I learned, and the difficulties encountered in attempting to emulate truly remarkable leaders. I believe that a full understanding of these particular values is essential for anyone attempting to master this elusive and sometimes mysterious process—or art—of leadership.

LEADERSHIP VALUES

The Fourteen Values that I will address are:
- INTEGRITY
- VISION
- DECISIVENESS
- SELF-DISCIPLINE
- ACCOUNTABILITY
- OPTIMISM
- COURAGE
- HONESTY
- TRUSTWORTHINESS
- PRIDE
- COMPASSION
- LOYALTY
- HUMILITY
- ENLIGHTENMENT

Each value will be defined and hopefully offer some fresh insight on exactly how that particular value relates directly to leadership. Additionally, for each value, I have included a personal story in which I believe that specific value is personified, or in some cases, *not* personified.

These values are based on my perspective and forty years of organizational leadership experiences with the Philadelphia Fire Department. No doubt, other writers may have very different opinions and probably a different number than fourteen.

AN INTROSPECTION

Additionally, each of these Fourteen Values are closely interrelated. For example, how can you maintain your integrity if you don't have the value of courage? How can you relentlessly pursue a positive vision for the future unless you possess the value of self-discipline?

It's also necessary to point out that every one of these values has an opposite behavior—a flip side. Each "good" value comes with an antonym. That's the amazing and extremely challenging thing about leadership. In so many ways, high-quality, effective leadership is all about having the right values that lead directly to making the right personal *choices*. We know this because some leaders:

- are immoral—they possess little or no integrity.
- can never make a timely decision.
- lack the required self-discipline.
- flee from any accountability.
- prefer viewing the world as a half-empty glass.
- are devoid of any meaningful vision.

Sadly, we also have some leaders who:

- boast incessantly.
- lack any type of courage.
- flaunt their arrogance daily.
- find it difficult to be honest.
- demonstrate zero trustworthiness.
- demand loyalty—but never extend any.
- exist contentedly in their own dimly lit world.
- think that showing any compassion is a sign of weakness.

LEADERSHIP VALUES

Staying true to your positive values is the rudder that steers you toward correct decisions. Many leaders do not make the right choices simply because they have the wrong values. Values and choices are strongly and irrevocably linked together. For most of us, the two are a package deal.

I am sure that you know of some co-workers who are technically able to perform the boss's job. They can adequately fulfill the role, complete the tasks, and get the work out. But that doesn't make them a genuine leader—not a *real* leader; that's a totally different skill set.

If effective, high-quality, visionary, value-driven leadership was that easy, there would not be this proliferation of workshops, seminars, and formal, structured academic programs to "learn" leadership skills. Here is just a partial list of college degrees in my area that offer a bachelor's or master's degree in some form of leadership. These are programs in which the word "leadership" actually appears in the degree's title:

- Educational Leadership
- Financial Leadership
- Global Environmental Leadership
- Instructional Leadership
- Museum Leadership
- Non-profit Organizational Leadership
- Organizational Leadership
- Strategic Leadership
- Urban School Leadership

AN INTROSPECTION

Obviously, if leadership is to be performed correctly, there must be a lot to learn.

THE INTROSPECTION COMPONENT

That brings me to the "Introspection" aspect of the Fourteen Values chapters. I'm hoping that you will contemplate the ideas and then honestly evaluate where you personally stand in relation to that value. The primary goal of this book is to help, even in some small way, to make *you* a better leader by helping you answer the questions:

- How are *you* doing?
- Are *you* missing the mark in modeling a given value?
- Do *you* need to improve your behavior at work or at home?

You might run through four or five values in a row feeling very comfortable with your leadership effectiveness, and then, out of nowhere, a leadership issue will arise which you never thought of in your entire career. The good news is that any introspection you perform will be totally private. This book comes with no formal self-evaluation forms; any personal introspection and behavioral modifications that you perform will be done *by* you, *for* you.

WORDS OF CAUTION

There are some potential limitations to your full appreciation and acceptance of this information.

First, the Fourteen Values are presented in brief, snapshot form; I do not explore in great depth the complex dimensions of each value.

LEADERSHIP VALUES

Each value could be, and has been, expanded enough to fill many scholarly volumes.

Secondly, if you are expecting scientific, technical, or purely academic information on all the different leadership theories and styles, you will be disappointed. My focus, especially with the personal stories, is geared toward the practical application of leadership—doing it. And, hopefully, doing it effectively.

Thirdly, there may be differences of opinion. During my career in the Fire Department, forty-nine firefighters died "in the line of duty." That was my reality. Forty-nine firefighters reported in for roll call—and never returned home! And, as I rose through the ranks, the stakes, the responsibility, this "leadership factor"—kept getting higher and more serious with each successive promotion. And, very quietly, almost subconsciously, "life or death" became one of my personal yardsticks for measuring the impact or importance of life's events. I mention this in case you and I differ in relating to the upcoming values.

Some of my thoughts might surprise you because I discuss some issues that do not routinely surface in a formal leadership training classroom setting. So, why bring them up? Because these are exactly the kinds of things that I wish somebody would have told me as I was ascending the leadership ladder.

So much of what you will read on these pages, I had to learn the hard way. This platform is great for me because I can speak freely, from my heart. There are no agendas or party lines to influence any of my comments. The words all fall squarely on me; they are truly my experiences, my thoughts, and my beliefs.

Lastly, there may be some leadership values and issues that you think are incredibly important that I believe are insignificant, and vice versa. There may be leadership values and issues to which you never give a second thought, that I think are everything. Either way, keep in mind that just as attending a course on Ethics won't magically transform you into an ethical person, the same holds true for reading this book. There is an enormous difference between *understanding* these Fourteen Values—and *living* them

Will my observations rock your world with new and exciting leadership revelations? I doubt it. But the Fourteen Values may get you to think about the subject matter in a new and deeper way. To have a reader put down a chapter, reflect a bit, and think, "Hmm, I never really looked at it that way before" would delight and humble this writer. To know that somewhere, someday, a future or current leader would read something in these pages that alters an individual or organizational outcome in a truly positive way—that would make all my efforts worthwhile.

UNDERSTANDING PERSONAL VALUES

The dictionary defines a value as "a principle standard or quality considered inherently worthwhile or desirable." The root for the word is *valor* (from the stem of the Latin word *Valere*), which means strength. That's why when we run across, or tangle with, a seemingly strong-minded person, we sometimes have to look no further than his or her values to understand what's going on and what we're up against.

Our values are the deep-seated, pervasive standards that influence almost every aspect of our lives. They are deeply held views on what we find most worthwhile and they reflect our personal "standards of worth" in what should, or should not, be. Often our values are deeply submerged in our subconscious. They can be so deep-seated that we act unconsciously, as if we are on autopilot.

Because our personal values are so deep and emotionally bound, they are often difficult to change. But this character rigidity that emanates from our value system can, and frequently does, act as a source of enormous internal strength. Our value system can be "the rock" or the "true north" that provides us with the motivation to take action, keep going, or just do the right thing.

Each of us creates our own values by the meanings that we attach to things and events. These meanings then translate into what we believe are worthwhile thoughts and behaviors and become our values. Frequently, these values are embedded so deeply within us that they end up becoming our own social norms. We act in a specific fashion because we know it is, or just feels, right for us.

I once had a professor who said, "Human beings are meaning-making machines who go through every day making judgment after judgment, sometimes very rapidly and with little or no thought." He pointed out that we are all hardwired that way and it's very difficult for us to reduce these endless lightning-quick daily judgments. He

AN INTROSPECTION

advised that we are in a constant judgmental state: "That's good; That's bad; He's a nitwit; She's pretty cool."

We all create our own personal value system of what is important to us; we even create individual layers of importance. In our minds, other people adhering to our value system becomes our personal "rules of the game." And, when someone breaks one of our important personal rules of the game, even if we do not overtly react, an alarm goes off because we notice all "violators" of our personal value system. Most times, we do not like it.

What is one of your top personal rules of the game? Can you name a specific behavior from another person that immediately triggers your "violation alarm"? For me, it's being disrespected—especially by someone who doesn't even know me.

Very importantly, our informal, yet powerful, individual values serve to let us know how we are to operate on a daily basis. They act as our behavioral boundaries while we are in public or behind closed doors. Very rarely will we need a rulebook, guideline, code of conduct, or a standard operating procedure (SOP) to figure out if someone is out-of-bounds. We just know it.

Values can change in individuals, organizations, and even in countries; but it's rarely an overnight shift. Think about your own values; are they drastically different than they were ten years ago? Probably not.

LEADERSHIP VALUES

Although values are related to beliefs and principles, they are not the same thing. Together, the three "systems" help us to make decisions, both smaller ones, and life and death.

Values differ from beliefs in one important way. Many times, even if it takes a while, beliefs can be proven or disproven. For example, people used to believe without question that the earth was both flat and the center of the universe. These beliefs were, of course, proven to be incorrect. Our individual values are different because they cannot be scientifically proven correct or incorrect.

Values also differ from principles in several ways. Among them:

- Values are social norms created by men and women; principles are more of natural law.
- Values are emotional; principles are factual.
- Values are personal; principles are impersonal.
- Values are subjective; principles are objective.
- Values are arguable; principles tend to be self-evident.

Our values provide us with a set of organized principles that assist us in living our lives. Therefore, what is most important for us to accomplish in our public and private lives can often be described in relation to the values we hold. In other words, even our goals can be directly connected to our value system.

Remain aware that not all human values must be good. I learned first-hand that many bad people have strong values too. These people (leaders?) can also possess deeply held views on what type of behavior is acceptable and worthwhile. Their twisted value system can just as easily serve to assist them in achieving their unethical, offensive, or sinful goals.

Sometimes, people mistakenly think of values as a series of "should or should nots"; rules for what we can or cannot do. This is a very limited approach to appreciating the immense importance of our individual value system. That's because our personal values can be energizing, motivating, and inspiring—all at once. When we care passionately about something, we value it. And, when we value something, it can spur us on to great achievements. The highest achievements of people *and* organizations arise when they feel inspired to accomplish something that fits their highest values.

CHAPTER 1

Integrity

LET'S BEGIN OUR INDIVIDUAL VALUES "JOURNEY" WITH INTEGRITY. After all, if you are not willing to "do the right thing" consistently, not many of your other admirable values will even matter.

In the simplest of terms, integrity is moral soundness. At its foundation is a strong sense of what human behavior is right, and equally important, what is wrong. By soundness, I mean that one's level of integrity is free of defects and cannot be easily shaken. True values do not change direction with every new breeze, no matter how strong that breeze may be.

Integrity is about doing what is right—no matter what. You can't be experiencing a rough shift every other week in which your integrity level drops off to meet the dilemmas. Personal integrity should have no ebb and flow. It's not something you alter based on a particular situation or challenge.

LEADERSHIP VALUES

When you are a person of integrity, people notice you. People notice you because you live your life guided by principles that compel you to continually take the high road in this grand adventure that we call life. When you have integrity, you care more about doing the right thing than doing "things" right. You care more about sticking to your values than looking good.

I have known newly promoted leaders who assumed it would be easy to maintain their integrity in their new roles. They must have truly believed that there's a shortage of situations—and people—out there who are just waiting to challenge or test their leadership ability. When asked, I usually caution them that some of their greatest challenges may come from people who they thought were their genuine friends.

An appointment to a leadership position may force some leaders to jettison some of these so-called friends so they can operate in their new environment. Dare I say it? Sometimes, the biggest impediment to achieving our full leadership potential is the company that we keep. The reality is that we are judged, at least to some degree, by the company we keep.

And those judgments are frequently notable in evaluating a leader's off-hours associations. When it's not strictly company time or business related, leaders *do* have a personal choice with whom they associate. People do notice who the boss hangs out with.

When asked, I remind newly promoted leaders to recognize and, if necessary, make any required post-promotion "friendship

AN INTROSPECTION

adjustments." Many newer leaders have to go through this painful detachment phase to reach their true potential. Detachment can be agonizing; who wouldn't want to hang out with Crazy Dave or Shotgun Susie?

Let me give you the bad news in attempting to be a leader with integrity. Integrity comes with a "price tag." Sooner or later, as a leader, you have to pay up; and it works in an odd way. In most organizations, the more you care, the sooner you are likely to have to pay the price.

The price tag of trying to be a person, or especially a leader, of integrity can be very high. It's a high price because often there are:

- confrontations.
- sleepless nights.
- migraine headaches.
- knots in your stomach.
- rumors, half-truths, and lies told about you.
- the loss of the artificial friends we discussed.
- days in which you may wake up and wish that you never took the promotion in the first place.

But your integrity is so important as a leader; and it's definitely worth fighting for. For on the leadership scale, there is no higher value than consistently doing the right thing.

LEADERSHIP VALUES

WHAT ARE SOME CHALLENGES TO MAINTAINING YOUR INTEGRITY?

Not understanding—or accepting—that you need to bat a perfect 1.000

One reason that leaders can have a difficult time maintaining their integrity is that the standard is almost always perfection. Winning the "Integrity Game" is not a best-of-seven scenario, nor does it give you points for all your vast previous admirable behavior. Maintaining your integrity is always about *today*—this situation, this moment.

A leader can usually recover quickly and fully from a poor operational or administrative decision. But integrity is different. If you make a decision that clearly indicates a lack of integrity on your part, it reveals your true character to those observing and following you. These types of decisions are extremely difficult to make excuses for and recover from. Lapses in your integrity will be major events to your bosses, peers, subordinates, stakeholders, and the public. Even to your friends.

If one was to equate maintaining your integrity to a competitive game, I think it would most resemble a single-elimination tournament. As a leader, just one "loss" of your integrity could equal a career-defining (ending?) moment.

Maybe you can bat .500 by demonstrating some personal positive values and still be on the all-star team; but anything less than a perfect score in handling integrity issues will eventually scuttle all your leadership goals and aspirations. There might be another "tournament" for you, but it will not be in the near future.

And even if you survive the negative experience and are fortunate enough to appear in the "leadership arena" at a later time, your loss of integrity will be a well-known matter of record that is extremely difficult to dismiss.

Weakening during prolonged integrity trials

Unfortunately, your sudden personal or organizational challenges are not a planned component of your life or workload; you can't space them out. Occasionally, challenges to your integrity will come at you in bunches. Sometimes, correctly making one huge integrity decision just brings about even more challenges of equal or higher anguish.

These successive challenges are much more difficult to handle than singular, spaced-out events, and can make for a very emotional, excruciating week, month, or period of time. But, it is very important to recognize the "Integrity Cyclone" when you are in it. The key to success is to remember that eventually things will settle down and even out. And, with that recognition and confidence, a leader can dig even deeper within to emerge from that very challenging period with an integrity grade of a solid "A."

Seeking constant praise for your actions

The dilemma here is that doing the right thing—acting with integrity—occasionally requires you to keep silent on your actions. Even when your decision or action is full of wisdom and righteousness, there are occasional circumstances when blowing your own horn, telling it like it is, or simply letting people know the facts, can be counterproductive for others. Maintaining silence and restraint can be a problem if you're a leader who loves all the attention and reinforcement that your guidance brings.

True leadership requires one to resist any urge to cheapen moments of demonstrated integrity with the need to have your ego stroked. Get used to it: acting with genuine integrity, day in and day out, can occasionally remove any headliner/center stage status you enjoy and quietly place you in a back row temporarily. If you are constantly craving a desire for praise and validation, you are going to spend some uncomfortable time squirming in that back row.

I have found that people who exhibit consistent integrity do not display the desire, or need, to train the spotlight on themselves, or to have someone else illuminate their outstanding character. They feel that who they are should be quite evident to everyone.

Believing a bad situation can't get worse

I have attended my share of high-level, crisis meetings in which the prevailing mood was that the situation at hand could not possibly get any worse. We/I would be told something like, "If we could all just stand tall and work together for the next forty-eight hours, the worst will be behind us."

AN INTROSPECTION

I found this approach to be both helpful—yet also naïve. Yes, it served to rally and focus us; but, it also presented us with a false bottom threshold of bad news. Our leadership incorrectly felt that they knew everything about the problem. But, they couldn't possibly know all the dimensions, depths, and trajectories of the problem because things were unsettled and happening much too fast.

In my crisis management travails, I have found that it's not difficult or uncommon for any bad situation to get worse—in the blink of an eye. Effective leadership requires this realistic insight because if the situation does get worse, your reliance on personal integrity may even be that much more important.

Discovering that the right course of action is not that clear

It's a lot easier to maintain your integrity if you at least know, or feel, what the right thing to do is. However, sometimes a leader can find him or herself compelled to choose between two genuinely bad options; both alternatives can be equally unpleasant.

I have not discovered a perfect one-size-fits-all answer or process when forced to select one of two poor options. However, some points that serve me well when I'm not sure in which direction to proceed, yet I know that something must be done, are:

- Most of the time, you'll obtain a better outcome if you select and implement the least bad option quickly. This is because (1) not making any decision frequently allows the status quo

to deteriorate, and (2) selecting the lesser of two evils later may be too late. Inaction is often an integrity killer.
- Be keenly aware of, and account for, the emotional stress that you may be under. Do your best to honestly factor in your emotional state, knowing it can strongly affect your reasoning.
- Try to gain some clarity by envisioning the *specific* details and events that will unfold for each of your choices once your decision sets things in motion.
- IF time permits, try to create a third (or fourth, or fifth) option.
- Rely on your intuition and gut feeling.

Keep in mind, that no matter how hard you attempt to imagine an outcome, *all* the ramifications of your decision will remain truly unknown until you implement it.

My Additional Advice on Maintaining Integrity

Stay strong—no matter what. Don't allow yourself to even entertain weak thoughts. Challenge any inner demons pushing you to abandon your integrity. Once you give in morally, it'll be easier the next time.

Upgrade the character of your immediate friends and team. Actively seek out and, where possible, surround yourself with men and women of sterling character and strong positive values. Associating with

AN INTROSPECTION

high-quality people who you respect and admire often provides an extra incentive to do the right thing.

Maintain a role model's guidance. Ask yourself, "What would Chief Richmond do?" What would _____ (your choice) _____ do? NOTE: William C. Richmond was a legendary Philadelphia Firefighter who rose through the ranks to become the fire commissioner from 1984 through 1988. He spent his entire life living all the values described in this book and is remembered as an extraordinary leader.

Feel your failure. Go beyond any visualization of failure and try to actually *feel* the shame, the embarrassment, and the remorse of your planned action—your loss of integrity.

THE DEVIL'S RECRUITMENT TEAM

Sister Bridget, of the Sisters of the Immaculate Heart of Mary Order, is one of my favorite people on the planet; she came into my life at a time when I was questioning the reason for my existence. In our first conversation, she advised me that it was going to be very difficult to find the correct answers if I couldn't even formulate the right questions.

This fiftyish, blue-eyed, strong-willed woman, with the short gray hair, regaled in the blue habit and the large silver crucifix hanging around her neck, took my best punches aimed

LEADERSHIP VALUES

at her beliefs—and always ended up "knocking me out" with some type of a thought-provoking comment that stopped me in my tracks.

A few years back, a small group of us were talking to Sister Bridget following a meeting in the rectory basement of Saint George Church. Sister surprised a few of us by acknowledging that being a nun probably makes it a lot easier to stay on the straight and narrow than the lay population. She said that living the very structured religious life provided far fewer diversions and temptations. She acknowledged having fewer opportunities to even cross over to the dark side.

Sister Bridget was genuinely curious to know how each of us cope with the voluminous daily temptations in life. As we replied in turn with our personal philosophies on how to become and remain a good person, I noted her pensive facial expressions and uncomfortable body language at our responses.

Upon our completion she said, "Let me tell you a story, because I think that I spot a common theme in all of your approaches to life's challenges."

Sister began, "One day, the Devil decided to increase the intake numbers down in Hell, so he summoned all his executive vice-presidents in charge of recruitment. He addressed the high-level recruiters who were all gathered in a big boardroom reviewing the disappointing intake charts. The Devil was upset; there just weren't enough people going to Hell."

AN INTROSPECTION

I smiled at this visual and Sister Bridget continued, "The Devil started the meeting by proclaiming, 'I want to raise the next quarter's intake numbers by 25%.' With that announcement, the recruiters went crazy. They were so upset and moaned, whined, and shouted that they were already maxed out. The recruitment team executives assured the Devil that they were working around the clock to maximize their efforts in sending people to Hell."

Sister pulled us deeper into her story by quoting the angry Devil, "Hold on; you're forgetting these humans' unlimited capacity for one thing. It's the fundamental weakness that allows them to quite easily relinquish their integrity."

The Devil then appealed to the recruiters' vast experience, "Listen, it's not going to be a lot of extra work for us; their greatest failure mechanism is already in place. We won't have to be up there actually twisting arms to bring them down here. All we have to do is provide more decision opportunities for them. Just give them more challenges to do the right thing. Believe me, they won't disappoint us. We have history on our side."

Sister continued speaking animatedly as the Devil, "Look, these human beings have at least one built-in sophisticated process that frequently prevents them from doing the right thing. Most of them regularly utilize this amazing process that eases and sometimes completely erases any of their deserved

LEADERSHIP VALUES

embarrassment, guilt, or shame. The majority of people don't even know they're doing it."

Then she turned to me, "Gary, what human capacity or weakness of ours that can often prevent some people from doing the right thing was the Devil alluding to? Can you guess?"

"I have no idea, Sister," I replied.

"RATIONALIZATION! Gary. Plain old rationalization."

"Rationalizing can send me to Hell, Sister?"

"Well, I think it can sure detour your journey to Heaven. And, it's so easy to do. We hear people rationalize every day. It's very difficult to maintain our integrity 100% of the time because we can rationalize issues, events, and even our own behavior. We're capable of rationalizing just about anything."

Sister elaborated, "Have you ever heard someone say 'I'm working so hard here at the office and I get no appreciation. So, I'm *entitled* to take some of these stationery supplies home for my personal use'?

"Or, how about this one, 'Do I fudge the numbers at work? Sure, I do, but so does everybody else. Lying is part of the organizational culture around here. You *have* to lie just to stay even.'"

She then turned it on me again, "Can you think of a similar example, Gary?"

"Come to think of it, yeah," I replied, "yesterday, a friend who works in sales said to me, 'I was skipped over during the last round of promotions and I know that nobody deserved it

AN INTROSPECTION

more than me. So, if I add some mileage to my reimbursement tab and a few items to my expense account, what's the big deal? These people *owe* me!'"

Sister Bridget smiled broadly and said, "Perfect; can you see it? Your friend was rationalizing stealing money."

"I can see that you're making a connection between personal integrity and rationalizing."

"You're right, Gary," replied Sister, "and that connection is a straight line. Rationalization is so damaging to our integrity because it helps us to avoid looking at the true explanation for our behavior. When we rationalize, we substitute a safe and reasonable explanation—as we see it—for the true cause of our behavior."

"This sounds pretty deep, Sister," I said.

"It can be, Gar', very deep indeed. Freud called rationalization one of our 'psychological defensive mechanisms.' He observed that when we rationalize, it can be a conscious act, or it can be a subconscious life-long *habit*."

I was a little disappointed, "So, I can't rationalize anymore, Sister?"

She continued to educate me, "Sure, you can. An appropriate dose of rationalization is not a bad thing for any of us. Psychologists tell us that a certain amount of rationalizing is essential in getting through our daily struggles. Rationalizing reduces anxiety, maintains our important self-esteem, and reestablishes our valuable inner peace. But, like most things in life, too much of it can become a big problem."

"How do I know when I'm rationalizing too much, Sister?" I asked.

"Well, now, that's the real heart of the problem; knowing when you've gone past an appropriate healthy level. I can tell you that first you have to truly understand the concept and the power of rationalization. And, after you understand it, you then must be constantly on the alert for its overuse."

Sister Bridget explained further, "I'm sure that there are a lot of different successful methods out there to control rationalization, Gary. But I think it begins with you honestly evaluating your decisions and feelings to see if any of them are distorting reality. Secondly, and most importantly, are those distortions actually causing you any real-world problems?"

I measured my words, "So, it begins with me being totally honest with myself?"

"Yes. And, that's not easy for many of us."

Sister then stopped talking. I think she correctly sensed that in our brief exchanges, she had accidentally identified—more like sledge hammered—an embarrassed life-long practitioner of rationalization: me.

She offered me one of her warm smiles and extended her hand for me to grasp. I took it and just gave one of those minimal

AN INTROSPECTION

affirmative nods without saying a word. We both knew what had just happened.

Sister Bridget's continued kindness toward me throughout the years was overwhelming. But no other kindness ever rivaled the meaningfulness of that brief conversation during which she held up a "mirror" for me to reflect on so many of my decisions and beliefs.

I took her advice. I wanted (needed!) to know much more about how rationalization could both help and hurt me. After a while, I even came to recognize some of my personal early warning signs that I might be headed toward overuse. I made the following two observations:

First, did I *always* feel this way about the person or the issue? Or, was I just using a timely *excuse* that I'd recently invented to allow myself to yield to some personal weakness? My experience with rationalizing is that it frequently comes with an expiration date. What happens for me is that, whether it's one moment, one night, one week, or one month, I embrace this new thought, belief, or emotion for just enough time for me to do the wrong thing. So, tip #1: if it's a newly acquired belief or justification that is seemingly coming in from your personal "left field"—be careful!

Secondly, if you find that you must work at accepting this newly acquired belief or justification—that it's not coming to you naturally—it could be because it's outside of your true,

LEADERSHIP VALUES

time-tested personal value system. Tip #2: if you sincerely believe the thought or feeling is right, then it shouldn't be such an effort for you to embrace.

Since that day, I have come a long way in understanding and controlling my human tendency toward rationalization. Sister Bridget was right; it's not that easy. But my awareness and understanding of rationalization has proven very valuable in attempting to be an effective leader. I know that I shouldn't, but sometimes I feel lucky when I'm in the company of championship-level rationalizers. I feel like I've somehow been blessed with an important piece of the leadership puzzle that they don't possess: I can see the truth; I can see reality.

Integrity is everything.

PHOTO COURTESY OF THE PHILADELPHIA FIRE DEPARTMENT

AN INTROSPECTION

INTROSPECTION

- So, within your personal introspection, what grade would you give *yourself* on integrity? Perfect? High? Improvement needed?

- Can you *always* be counted upon to do the right thing?

- Have you ever truly wanted to do the right thing on an integrity issue, but you let someone talk you out of it? Exactly why did that happen?

- Is there any disparity between your professional integrity and the way you conduct your personal life? Some leaders exhibit a dual-life; they have a "Dr. Jekyll—Mr. Hyde scenario" working. That's a problem because integrity doesn't come with an "On-Off" switch.

- As a leader, do you remember ever paying a price, that is, really getting beat-up for being a person of integrity? Did you come away thinking that integrity is really overrated? Or, can you still recall that deep personal satisfaction that accompanies some of our most shining human moments? Those are moments in which our personal integrity is severely challenged, yet, we manage to stand tall—no matter what.

CHAPTER 2

Vision

TO LEAD PEOPLE BEGS THE QUESTION: lead them *where*? Just where is it that you want to take your followers?

The leader's vision is a picture or a mental image of the future that the leader wants to create. But it's not just any picture; it's the *idealized state* (Bennis and Nanus, 1985). It is what things would look like if they were perfect, or close to it. Visions are so important to leaders because they allow them to picture excellence and then, most importantly, chart a course to required change.

The vision becomes the leader's expectation of the best possible future for the unit, office, group, practice, franchise, or for the entire organization—or, for the country.

So, where does a leader get a vision from? Usually, the leader's vision arises from multiple origins such as experience, facts, opportunities, challenges, dangers, disappointments, intuition, and certainly—hopes and dreams. With or without his/her eyes open, the leader should be able to actually see and describe this idealized state. Actively pursuing your own vision or being totally on-board with another person's vision can be an exhilarating and rewarding experience.

Although visions must be rooted in today's reality and what's going on now, *all visions focus on the future.* This focus must be specific—how to make things better a month from now, a year from now, or for a future generation. Understand that not all visions must be as lofty as eliminating world hunger; leaders can have smaller, less dramatic idealized states. Maybe your leadership vision is just working toward creating a harmonious, highly effective team at the office, the loading dock, or the school district.

The first vision you form on a future issue is usually not the precise finished version; frequently, you'll be required to make modifications along the way. So many leadership visions that are brought to life require a methodical process that forces one to learn new things, deal with surprises, overcome obstacles, and show flexibility, all while constantly moving toward the idealized state. I have discovered that in attempting to achieve a vision, patience is often your most valuable ally.

Vision works primarily within an organization, division, or group's emotional and spiritual resources to motivate and inspire followers. Because of this, the leader with a vision is operating on a different plane than the manager. As a contrast, the manager is usually focused on the processes, administration, productivity and/or performance of the organization, division, or group. In short: leaders tend to spend more time than managers in challenging, influencing, motivating, inspiring and communicating with others.

Many years ago, I attended a leadership conference for newly promoted first-level supervisors. I recall someone asking the instructor, "How can we clarify the distinctions between a leader and a manager?"

The instructor replied with this memorable offering: he told them to think about the difference between a train's conductor and its engineer. He stressed the importance of understanding their different roles on the team. The instructor equated the train conductor to the manager. It's this person's job to ensure that tickets are processed, everyone has a seat, the baggage is properly stowed, the food is on board, the sleeping berths are readied, etc.

However, the train engineer, acts more as a leader by being focused on the destination—where the passengers are actually headed. The instructor pointed out that the engineer was the one who took responsibility for everyone's safety, paid attention to timeframes, knew when to speed up or slow down, and even when to switch tracks.

Here are a few more common distinctions that serve to clarify the differences (Nanus, 1995):

- Managers administrate; leaders innovate.
- Managers primarily control people; real leaders inspire people.
- Managers are usually imitating someone else; leaders spend significant time actually creating.

AN INTROSPECTION

- Managers readily accept the status quo; genuine leaders frequently challenge it.
- Managers are usually focused on the bottom line; authentic leaders are focused on a different line: the horizon.

Remember that leading and managing are not mutually exclusive; I've seen many people who can perform both functions very well. One distinction that I can make is that all the truly outstanding leaders that I've been around have had at least some managerial capabilities. However, I've seen many managers without an ounce of leadership ability. My observations just serve to reinforce the notion that leading and managing are comprised of very different qualities, abilities, and skills.

Usually, implementing one's vision is a journey. Actually, many textbooks tell us that visioning is really a process. Probably like you, I've had some worthwhile visions I've been lucky enough to see turn into reality. And, I've had some that crashed and burned.

So, I can share with you what did work for me. These ten points have successfully guided me in reaching an idealized state time after time, in one situation after another. However, my experience never duplicated the suggested textbook process of completing one step and then neatly moving on to the next step. My visioning journeys always required me to be active in multiple process steps simultaneously. I was always going back and forth between sharing, selling, reinforcing, seeking buy-in, etc.; that's why I prefer the term *points* versus *steps*. Arranged in loose order, these ten points are what did work for me:

LEADERSHIP VALUES

GFA'S TEN POINTS OF VISION ACHIEVEMENT

1. **Introduce your vision.** After your research and preparation, your first goal should be to gather your team and formally lay out your idealized state in general terms. Don't insult people by spoon-feeding them your vision a little bit at a time, or worse, by surprising them. During this introduction stage, and throughout the process, nothing will be more important than your ability to listen to ALL those impacted by your vision.

2. **Share your vision.** It's important to share your vision with everyone who will listen. If your vision is to work effectively, its best chance comes from the widest possible distribution. Think about your imagined idealized state as the picture on the outside of a 500-piece jigsaw puzzle box. Can you imagine the difficulty your 5 or 100-person unit would encounter working toward putting the puzzle (your vision) together if you're the only one who ever saw the finished picture on the outside of the box?

3. **Sell your vision.** (NOTE: Many times, I combined this activity with the initial introduction.)

    Selling your vision doesn't mean that you ram it down everyone's throat. I've found that even if your vision is good, you'll limit positive results by using edict, threats, coercion, and/or exercising your power. Ideally, the benefits of your vision will speak for themselves.

    Another caution: because selling is an interpersonal activity that can stir strong emotions, you may be better off framing your

AN INTROSPECTION

vision around "organizational issues" rather than moral principles. Why? Because people may react negatively to what they perceive as your judgment of their character and/or values.

This selling phase must include you formally addressing the issue of "Why?" You must describe what you see as the problem, dilemma, or challenge and why change is necessary. It's important throughout the selling process that you model the behavior of a change agent, not a complainer.

Try to get those around you to accept the vision as a common purpose that will benefit everyone. It is vital that everyone sees how *they* fit into *your* mosaic, so be prepared to answer the question: "What's in it for me/us?" Because you need their commitment, take the time to explain the "history" of your vision and exactly why you feel so strongly about the required change or new direction.

In this early phase, if you choose, it's okay to stick to the "big picture" elements of your vision. Details and minutiae can be revealed later at the buy-in stage.

Most importantly, you should provide (i.e. sell) the inspiration that builds a solid coalition around your vision. And, if final approval is above your authority level, of course, you'll also be required to sell the vision to your boss (or bosses).

Successfully selling your vision is often difficult, so never lose sight of the fact that a significant part of selling your vision—is selling yourself. Did you know that research indicates that 70% of all organizational change efforts fail? So, the odds of your vision succeeding are not in your favor.

4. **Provide vision clarity.** Make sure that your vision is clear to everyone. The easier that the vision is to understand, the easier it will be for you to communicate it. And, keep your vision in the language of the key stakeholders so they can understand, discuss, and evaluate it easily within their own circles and comfort level.

5. **Seek vision buy-in.** At this stage, you may have to tailor your pitch to a more detailed and focused message for the organization's decision-makers and all those having any legitimate influence over your vision's success. To successfully achieve buy-in, you need more than just their agreement with your vision; you need their commitment of time, energy, resources, and power.

Ideally, you want your team to take genuine ownership of your vision and to be in a true partnership with you. Your vision should not be a "rental" for them. After all: when was the last time you saw someone change the oil in a rental car?

Some research states that for your vision to be successful, you will need at least 75% buy-in from all those effected, so the more that you can demonstrate flexibility to allow your vision to become a "co-creation," the more likely the buyers are to feel vested in the outcome. Here, it's best that all your vision conversations contain the words "We, Us, and Our"; try not to refer to your vision from an "I, Me, or My" perspective.

AN INTROSPECTION

6. **Make your vision come to life.** Help others to see your vision as clearly as possible. Discuss it, articulate it, write it up, write it down, draw a picture or a flowchart, and/or show them a model or some photographs; it's true: a picture is worth a thousand words. Also, if you can, try to project the vision's application to present day issues and events.

7. **Reinforce your vision continuously.** From Day One, you should be reinforcing your vision through strategies and decisions that you make every day. As time goes on, this reinforcement should make your vision even stronger and clearer to everyone (Bennis and Nanus, 1985).

8. **Don't make decisions that run counter to your professed vision.** Understand the importance of the leader's everyday choices, which includes living the "little details." Everybody on the team is watching you, so if your behavior doesn't completely align with and support the vision, how will those under and around you embrace the change? You will have zero credibility—even if your vision is brilliant. Ralph Waldo Emerson summed up Point #8 perfectly: "What you do speaks so loudly, I can't hear what you're saying."

On a related point, I've seen leaders fall down when they think that their role is to remain focused solely on the big picture. They mistakenly believe that the little things always work themselves out through the efforts of those serving below them. This can be a costly mistake; sometimes a leader's inattention to the little things is what allows them to grow into major issues and thwart much more than a new vision.

9. **Keep everybody informed on your vision's progress.** Some leaders are working and thinking so hard about achieving tomorrow's vision that they forget to tell subordinates what's happening today. It's a common mistake, especially after you've worked so hard to get the group's buy-in. If you're the leader, you must keep the subordinates up to speed on the status of the vision by communicating regularly.

10. **Share credit for your vison's success.** This last point is important for any leader's long-term success in continuing to turn his/her visions into reality. Sadly, some leaders totally ignore this phase and then cannot understand why their team is reluctant to support any of their future visions.

   A true leader knows that sharing credit is an effective win-win strategy for everyone. The benefits for the subordinate or team include enhanced morale, increased self-confidence, and receipt of the leader's gratitude. A leader privately offering praise or giving due-credit clearly demonstrates the use of a positive leadership tool. However, private appreciation comments usually run a distant second in comparison to the value of public praise.

   Sharing credit also benefits a leader by providing evidence that shows that he/she is able to build a strong, effective team; a team that's much more likely to support future visions.

   But most importantly, the leader should share credit because it's just the right thing to do—period.

AN INTROSPECTION

So, what can a vision really do for a leader? Why is it so beneficial? Why is visioning studied so often in leadership development?

GFA'S SEVEN BENEFITS OF A LEADERSHIP VISION

In my experience, having a clear vision can:

1. **Act as the bridge from the present reality to the future.** If your picture of the future is powerful enough, you and your followers can actually cross over on it; the bridge can serve to transport all of you to a better tomorrow. I've always tried to build my vision bridges on the combined "structural elements" of facts, confidence, and optimism.

2. **Serve as a "mental map" to show you the way to a better place.** With this mental map (vision) in your head, it can serve as a compass which is constantly guiding you to where you want to go. If the vision is strong enough, its compass will keep you pointed in the right direction, even when you and your followers are struggling through periods of tough terrain.

3. **Bring everyone together.** Because their collective energy is now focused on the vision, your team can feel united, maybe for the first time, around a common cause or dream, and support and encourage each other.

4. **Empower your team.** When the group believes in your vision, they can feel empowered. And, their empowerment can lead to an increased urge, desire, or even commitment to act.

5. **Help everyone to make decisions *more on their own* than ever before.** This great benefit occurs because the vision has removed so

much of the organizational gray area and uncertainty. The group's destination is now crystal clear to everyone. This significantly reduces those frequent (killer) delays in which the team members must stop to check in, get approval, or ask for the leader's guidance. Their clarity and buy-in provides team members with a higher comfort level in making a decision when a discrepancy arises or taking a risk that clearly aligns with the leader's vision.

6. **Improve long-range planning.** Concentrating on your vision frequently enables you to *see* the sequential steps required to reach your idealized state. And, having this clarity allows you to better understand the needed resources, probable challenges, timeframe requirements, and more, that you will face during your journey.

7. **Highlight unsatisfactory employee behavior.** When your vision is firmly in place, it's much tougher for anyone on the team to lie down, skate by, or not pull his/her weight. A "bum" just stands out too much when everybody else is working hard and moving in the same direction. Lazy workers flourish in organizational fuzziness and darkness. The last person an indolent slug wants to be around is a leader with a clear vision—especially if the other team members buy into the leader's vision.

So, what's it like to actually work in an organization or unit that is devoid of any leadership vision? It's dark and depressing. Nobody (who matters) ever sees the light; month after month, workers just try to find their way through puzzling shades of continuous organizational darkness. They are not really going anywhere specific, unless you count going in circles a destination.

AN INTROSPECTION

I've known some so-called leaders who focus way too much on checking the unit's or organization's rear-view mirror. Certainly, it's worthwhile to periodically look back on positive events, but some leaders spend too much time looking backward only to relive and regret the negative past decisions and events. This backward focus drains some of the leader's valuable time and energy. I have found that our best leaders spend most of their time looking forward through the unit's/organization's windshield. These leaders are totally focused on the future, always asking: "Where are we going?"

Because visions are always about change, turning a leader's vision into reality can be a very challenging and emotional leadership experience. I've found that the hardest visions to bring to life are those which will require a change to the manner in which the group has been "doing it" for years, or decades. It seems to me that the longer the custom or procedure has been in place, the more difficult it will be to obtain total buy-in for your vision.

Most people dislike having change forced upon them, which isn't terribly surprising because routines provide daily stability to our lives. So, it should be no shock to you if your team initially resists your new vision. For them, your vision can directly trigger a fear of the unknown which can easily produce strong feelings of anxiety, tension, stress, and/or anger. This is yet another serious consideration underscoring the amount of thought required *before* attempting to lead your followers on any vision journey.

Let me conclude the value of leadership vision by very slightly modifying something that Michelangelo said 500 years ago: "The greater

LEADERSHIP VALUES

danger for most leaders is not that their aim is too high and they miss the target, but that it is too low and they reach it." That's exactly where many of today's leaders are—just settling for comfortable mediocrity, playing it safe. I urge you not to settle when faced with any leadership challenge or opportunity. Aim as high as you can—for as long as you can!

A SPECIAL PLACE

When I was transferred to the Fire Academy to be the Department's Director of Training, the timing seemed perfect. I was forty-six years old and had been with the PFD for twenty-six years. Coming off a 24-7, intense, and emotional three-and-a-half-year tour of duty as the PFD's Executive Officer, I needed a change. I was also fortunate to have predecessors at the Academy who'd done an excellent job in addressing the core aspects of both training and education.

However, a strong concern of mine upon arrival was the facility itself; I felt that the physical learning environment could better outwardly reflect all the meaningful campus activities.

My strong vision of what the Philadelphia Fire Academy could, and should, look like was centered on better displaying our heritage and values to all who set foot on the campus. I felt compelled to make the entire campus visually reflect, to the maximum degree possible, the soul of the PFD. For me, it was not enough for firefighters and visitors to know that the Fire

AN INTROSPECTION

Academy was a special place. My vision called for them to actually *see, touch, and feel* the heartbeat and legacy of our organization.

I introduced my vision in a meeting with Commissioner Roger Ulshafer and Deputy Commissioner Phil McLaughlin, two very forward-thinking top PFD leaders. I sold the benefits so well that they approved the vision on the spot. With their crucial blessing and support, I returned to the Fire Academy to begin a relentless sharing and selling of the vision and transformation that I could clearly see in my mind.

With the enthusiastic assistance of my always supportive Deputy Director Bill Shouldis and Operations Captain Bob Wolfe, I had vital Academy top staff buy-in immediately. Admittedly, there were a few junior officers on the Academy's assigned staff who were quite content with the status quo and resistant to any changes. But, in a few weeks, the sheer collective energy of the positive vision steamrolled over their eye-rolling, feet-dragging, and non-stop griping leaving them no choice but to get onboard or transfer out.

With the invaluable help of a great staff, both uniformed and civilian, and a very talented group of adjunct instructors, my vision began to come alive when, at my request, the Personnel Department officially changed the title of a probationary firefighter from "Recruit" to "Cadet." I believed strongly that cadet presented a more positive image—similar to the outstanding men and women serving at our Nation's military academies.

LEADERSHIP VALUES

The changes continued from there:

- The City's Streets Department made and installed new campus street signs with more meaningful titles such as "Dedication Drive," "Service Boulevard," (Ben) "Franklin Way," etc.
- Sixteen large blue and white flags with words indicating the PFD's Value System were prominently hung from poles on the side walls of the main auditorium.
- Colorful cadet class flags were hung in the Academy hallways to honor the members of every class who had previously passed through the hallowed halls.
- A large showpiece mural was designed, hand-painted by a PFD member (Dave Sweeney), and hung on the auditorium's front wall.
- A blue and white banner simply stating "March 15, 1871" was hung on the auditorium front wall commemorating the inception of our paid department.
- Large display cases containing PFD artifacts and memorabilia borrowed from the Fire Museum were installed in the main lobby.
- An assortment of antique, metal fire marks, signifying a building's specific fire insurance company, were mounted on walls.
- A huge fire scene photo was hung in the main lobby with the inscription: "You cannot choose your battlefield; the gods

AN INTROSPECTION

will do that for you. But, you can plant a standard, where a standard never flew."

- A PFD fire company patch collection was mounted in the reception area for all to see.
- Each graduating class was permitted to design and paint their own class mural, which would stand until the next graduating class, on one wall of the drill tower complex.
- Important additions were incorporated into the formal cadet curriculum such as: (1) *The origin and historical significance of the Firefighter Maltese Cross*, (2) *The Philadelphia Fire Department's Value System*, and (3) *Firehouse Etiquette*.
- Cadet graduation ceremonies were enhanced and lengthened to more accurately reflect the importance of the accomplishment, with more awards and recognition given to cadet achievements.
- Graduation ceremonies were moved off-campus to such larger, noteworthy venues as the University of Pennsylvania's Irvine Auditorium, Temple University's McGonigle Hall, Drexel University's Bluett Hall, the Bellevue Hotel, and other outstanding locations around the City.

Eventually, through my constant sharing, selling, clarifying, modifying, and reinforcing, and an enormous amount of help from others, my vision became a beautiful reality. Not just for me, but for the entire organization. If you were to visit the Philadelphia Fire Academy today, you would know that you

LEADERSHIP VALUES

had walked onto a unique location. And, without much effort at all, you could *see, touch, and feel* the heartbeat and legacy of a very special organization.

A VERY SPECIAL PLACE.

AN INTROSPECTION

0800 HOURS ROLL CALL.

PLATOON PRIDE.

LEADERSHIP VALUES

CONSTANT REMINDERS OF THE ORGANIZATIONAL VALUES AND EXPECTATIONS.

AN INTROSPECTION

HONORING THOSE WHO CAME BEFORE US.

LEADERSHIP VALUES

THE ORGANIZATION MOTTO.

THE BEGINNING—APPRECIATING OUR HISTORY.

AN INTROSPECTION

THE AUDITORIUM MURAL.

AN EMPHASIS ON FAMILY

LEADERSHIP VALUES

FIRE MARKS REMIND US OF OUR HERITAGE.

CLASS LEGACIES CONTINUE

AN INTROSPECTION

NEVER FORGOTTEN

GOD SPEED TO ALL OF YOU.

INTROSPECTION

- How do you feel you're doing using your ability and skills to create a vision?

- Do you currently have a clear personal or professional vision? Do you have some type of idealized state that you're journeying to?

- Is your vision a secret, or have you clearly articulated it to your key stakeholders? Is there any doubt that your team members clearly see your vision?

- Do you have the required buy-in from all your team members?

- How aware are you of your boss's vision? Are you onboard with his/her picture for the future?

- Do you have any problem sharing credit with others?

- Career-wise, are you working primarily with your organization's emotional and spiritual resources?

CHAPTER 3

Decisiveness

HOW IMPORTANT IS IT FOR A LEADER TO BE DECISIVE? To make those important timely and firm decisions before the ship sails and opportunity is lost—maybe forever? As a leader, if you can't pull the trigger on a big decision and be resolute about your decision, your strong integrity and inspiring vision for the future simply won't be relevant.

If you cannot make timely and effective leadership decisions, the truth is that your organizational presence won't matter much. Yep, you won't be that relevant! Here's an organizational truism that I've witnessed over and over: *Inaction can be as damaging to leadership as inept action.*

To me, making timely decisions seems to be connected to operating in your own comfort zone. Some leaders are comfortable deciding and committing early, while others struggle mightily within their narrow comfort zone and put it off as long as they can.

I once worked for a top staff executive (he was not a fireground commander; this behavior wouldn't fly on the street) who seemed to require a minimum of 99% of all the available information on an issue before he would green light anything. And, heaven forbid, if the decision involved interaction with another organization, he would hold out for the total 100% "informational package."

His office tables were filled with completed projects, along with all our staff recommendations; all he had to do was say "Yes" or "No." Sadly, he was incapable of offering a prompt decision. So, we spent an enormous amount of time *talking* about our organizational problems, challenges, and issues. It seemed that we were always preparing for a meeting, holding a meeting, or doing a post-meeting summary analysis. However, under the handcuffs of his indecisiveness, we very rarely actually did anything; we just kept discussing taking action.

That vision journey that we just discussed? It simply didn't exist for us. We all felt like we were just standing on a train platform, waving at other organizations passing us by—and wishing that we had a different leader.

Have you had a similar experience? What happens to the support staff and even down to the rank and file when the leader suffers "decisional paralysis"? The answer is: wide-spread organizational frustration. A large part of leadership is handling the natural anxiety that

AN INTROSPECTION

comes with making difficult decisions; quite frequently there's going to be some level of anxiety and/or stress on the leader.

I'll acknowledge that many of these opportunities that leaders mull over do involve some risk. But, remember this if you're the leader: "It's really difficult to steal second base—with your foot firmly planted on first base!" I hope this is not a news flash for you, but managing risk and tolerating anxiety and stress are fundamental and inescapable parts of most leadership roles.

Under the right conditions, a leader's *"Just do it—and contemplate later"* attitude definitely has merit. So much has been written and discussed about the benefits of organizations being agile by having "a bias for action." Tom Peters and Robert Waterman, authors of *In Search of Excellence*, popularized the term in describing how important it is "for successful organizations to stay spry, nimble, alert, and ready to act without the customary analysis or sufficient information."

I think that retired U. S. Army General Colin Powell offers even more meaty advice for us in his *Leadership Primer* with his formula of "P = 40–70." In this formula, "P" stands for probability of success and the numbers indicate the percentage of information needed. What this means is that we shouldn't act if we have only enough information to give us a less than 40% chance of being successful. Less than 40% is shooting from the hip and will cause you to make too many mistakes. But, we also shouldn't wait until we have enough facts to be 100% sure—because by then it will almost always be too late.

LEADERSHIP VALUES

The General cautions us that creating excessive delays in the name of "information gathering" breeds "analysis paralysis." Instead of reducing risk, we may actually be increasing it. He is very clear in his beliefs: once you have reached the 40% to 70% range of having all the available information, trust your intuition—go with your gut!

In *The 40–70 Rule*, Steven Anderson, Ph.D., further clarifies the General's formula: "People who want *certainty* in their decisions, end up working for other people."

I would add that if you find your leadership style has you continuously missing deadlines, revisiting analysis, and waiting for *everybody* to agree—your leadership effectiveness is in trouble.

To be a decisive leader, one must become relatively comfortable with making timely decisions and commitments. That means committing to ideas, to people, and to your own values. And you know that a commitment is a promise, pledge, or agreement in which you are bound to perform in a certain manner. Most organizations do not ask you to affirm your commitment aloud; most jobs don't require you to actually swear an oath. However, some of you, especially those in the military or public safety, are the exceptions. Your particular "call to duty" requires a commitment level that must stand at the very highest plateau.

Making a commitment is mostly an internal activity. A leader's commitment must be all-encompassing because it's a promise to the unit, to the subordinates, to the organization's leadership, to the organization itself, sometimes to the public, and always to his/her personal values. And that commitment must come from both your mind and your heart.

Regardless of our leadership experience, many of us could benefit from improved decision-making skills. And, these are several things that you can do, personally and professionally, to sharpen your decision-making processes:

- Participate in more tabletop exercises.
- Participate in more field exercises and drills.
- Study case histories and the lessons learned from past events.
- Discuss the decision-making process with your mentors and others you respect.
- Study, learn, and experiment with various problem solving and decision-making techniques such as Strengths, Weaknesses, Opportunities, and Threats (SWOT); Nominal Group Technique (NGT); Force Field Analysis; Cause and Effect Diagrams; etc. Ample information is available online describing these techniques.

Have you ever worked for a leader who consistently came up short making meaningful decisions and commitments? How about those leaders who commit to the aspects of leadership that they like or are good at, but pass on those aspects that don't appeal to or even frighten them? They may be the star of the office softball team and the unit's social director, yet they are so worried about their own popularity that they suffer from "supervisional paralysis." They cherish their popularity so much that they are afraid to upset anybody by making an unpopular decision; the thought of pissing people off scares them to death. Consequently, their leadership is weak and ineffective.

Let's face it: doing the right thing, fulfilling the leadership accountability role, demonstrating genuine integrity, and making the tough, timely decisions frequently make people angry. Accept it. As a leader, you're going to have to decide just how important your popularity is to you.

It is possible to be genuinely respected and liked by your subordinates. I have seen many highly effective leaders achieve it; they successfully walk that balance beam year-after-year, promotion-after-promotion. But they've got their priorities straight, and being popular isn't even near the top of their list. Their popularity is just a byproduct of their overall leadership excellence.

Do you want to know how to be popular as a leader? My advice is to try building your popularity on:

- Performing your own job in a very competent and faithful manner.
- Paying attention to the welfare and interests of your team.
- Being fair to everybody by never playing favorites.
- Being inflexible in demanding everyone's best efforts.
- Refusing to "carry" any bums; it's enormously unfair to all your good people.

A closing thought on decisiveness. In addition to a unit or organization decaying due to the leader's inaction, another, often unspoken, result of indecisiveness is frequently regret. Not just in your

AN INTROSPECTION

professional life; regret in your personal life too. Most of our regrets fall into one of two categories: either regrets about lost opportunities or regrets about relationships. Do you carry around a regret for an indecisive important moment that occurred recently? Two years ago? Twenty years ago?

From experience, I know that some of our regrets can actually cause our hearts to ache. I see similarities between regret and disease. You may be initially "infected" from an event in which you failed to make a timely decision and then promptly act on it. And, as you carry that memory around every day, the low-level ache may keep getting ever so slowly worse—while you do nothing about it. Then one day, you wake up, and you're 40, 50, or 60 years old and you've now contracted the full-blown disease. Hardly a day, a week, or a month ever passes without you experiencing the pain of regret. The memory of the results of your indecisiveness just won't go away. Now, sadly, in many cases, it really is too late to do anything about it.

Promise yourself that, no matter what, you won't look back on your leadership legacy and say, "I *really* wish I would have..." Make a decision—whatever it is.

GUT FEELING

On a night tour of duty, I responded as a fairly new deputy chief to an "all-hands working" fire in West Philly. When I arrived, the four engine companies and two ladder companies were coordinating an aggressive interior attack on a plumbing supply warehouse under the direction of two battalion chiefs. There was a moderate amount of fire somewhere in the center of the large one-story building.

As I stood on 62nd Street, observing and "commanding" the incident, I felt a strong, almost overwhelming, urge to withdraw the firefighters. I couldn't really put my finger on a specific reason to back everyone out; I just had an awareness that the operation didn't *feel* "right."

Rapidly, I mentally sought to find a legitimate reason to withdraw the fire attack teams, pull the second alarm, and transition to a safer exterior attack. But, I couldn't come up with any textbook reason to abandon the interior attack. The smoke wasn't pulsating or changing color; there were no signs of a flashover or backdraft; and the structure did not look like it was in imminent danger of collapse. I had nothing solid to pin my withdrawal on. I was afraid that if I did pull them out and nothing bad happened, that I would be labeled as "shaky"—and nobody wants to work for a shaky fire officer.

And then the building blew up.

I pulled the second alarm...then the third...then the fourth. Miraculously, no one was seriously hurt. Most of the force of the tremendous explosion—and accompanying huge fireball—went straight up into the clear night sky. It was truly frightening; I was glad they didn't subpoena my underwear.

AN INTROSPECTION

I felt horrible, and truly unworthy of commanding an entire firefighting division. I had chosen to ignore this strange, and uncommon for me, feeling—and firefighters could have been killed. Oddly enough, I received praise for the way I "handled" the event, which I think exacerbated my disappointment in myself.

Fortunately for me, the next morning at 0700 hours, I was to be relieved by one of my mentors and long-time heroes, a very experienced deputy chief who was enormously respected throughout the Department. I'll just say one thing about Teddy Roth and it'll tell you everything that you need to know: he was a young U. S. Marine in 1942 during the horrific six-month battle to take the island of Guadalcanal in the South Pacific.

I sat on the edge of the office bunk and told Teddy the entire story. He stood facing me and never interrupted; he clearly saw how low I was. The unforgettable wisdom he shared went something like this:

"Gar', God smiled on you last night; you're going to get a second chance. I know you studied hard and know a lot; but don't you see what happened out there? You completely ignored your gut feeling. No, that's not actually true; you *suppressed* your gut feeling to the point of inaction. These gut feelings that we occasionally get on the fireground occur spontaneously and are very difficult to explain at that particular moment. But they're nonetheless absolutely real. These gut feelings are trying hard to give us some type of guidance for the unknown. I know what you're talking about. It's happened to me several times."

The chief continued, "You have to learn that there's something coming from your subconscious—and it's trying desperately to bring you bits or pieces of information from experiences or knowledge that is *already* stored deep inside you. Our big problem is that the message is all scrambled and not crystal clear, like we want it."

He paused briefly to let me absorb the power of his message. Then Chief Roth turned the desk swivel chair to face me, sat down in it, and wheeled himself right in front of me and went even deeper.

"What's even worse is that these scrambled messages are usually occurring with lightning speed. As a chief officer, you gotta respect your gut feeling. You shouldn't overreact; but, for heaven's sake, don't ignore it completely."

"That's just what I did, Ted," I said, "I ignored the feeling completely."

"Gar', you have to understand that these messages and feelings are there for a reason. Remember that you're a highly trained professional; it's not like you were standing on 62nd Street observing from the perspective of a baker or a shoe-salesman. This is what you do for a living—you're a firefighter. You *thought* something was wrong. You *knew* it didn't feel right...

AN INTROSPECTION

and yet, you did nothing. Sometimes, in this profession, and in life itself, this is all we're gonna get: a gut feeling."

So, what were my eternal leadership learning points from that night?

- *Respect all your gut feelings.* Never completely ignore any strong gut feelings that surface in you; they're there for a reason. Even if you decide to take no action, at least consider or evaluate the feelings. But, don't completely ignore them.
- *Perform a "Two-second risk analysis."* To better evaluate whether you should act *immediately* on a gut feeling, ask yourself: What are the stakes? Is this gut feeling about selecting a new jacket, making an expensive purchase for your home—or is it a situation where someone may be harmed, injured, or killed?
- *Validate your leadership maturity.* Understand and accept that it's a lot easier to endure any negative label placed upon you, even unfairly, than to take on a devastating life-long regret because of your inaction.
- And, oh yes—remember that large plumbing supply warehouses may have some type of storage area for acetylene and other compressed gas cylinders.

Guess how many times after that night on 62nd Street that I completely ignored any strong gut feeling that arose in me?

LEADERSHIP VALUES

A4 The Bulletin Sunday, January 3, 1982 C

West Phila. plumbing firm burns

A four-alarm fire heavily damaged a West Philadelphia plumbing-supply company last night and forced several residents from their homes nearby, fire officials said.

Fire Commissioner Joseph Rizzo said two firefighters suffered minor facial burns while battling the fire and were treated at Lankenau Hospital.

The fire broke out at 7:15 p.m. in the D N Supply Corp., 62d and Media Streets, and was brought under control shortly before 9 p.m.

Rizzo said firefighters were able to contain the fire to the two-story brick-and-cement-block building. He said that the cause was under investigation and that no one was in the building at the time of the fire.

Policemen moved spectators back from the scene after several propane tanks inside the building exploded, shooting flames into the air. None of the nearby homes was damaged, and residents were evacuated as a precaution, fire officials said.

Bulletin Photo by Doug Scott
Firemen battle four-alarm blaze at DN Supply Company Inc.

Blaze guts 5 buildings of a West Phila. firm

By BRUCE E. BEANS
and LIN ZECHER-DALTON
Special to The Bulletin

A four-alarm fire gutted a plumbing supply warehouse complex in West Philadelphia last night, causing an estimated $750,000 in damage.

Fire officials evacuated seven families whose homes in the 6100 block of Media st. are located directly behind the warehouse.

Two Philadelphia firemen suffered minor injuries when an explosion ripped through DN Supply Co. Inc. at N. 62d and Media sts. They were hurt as they tried to enter the one of five buildings in the complex shortly before 7:30 P.M., officials said.

Firemen Robert Bianchi and Thomas Donovan of Engine Company 65 were treated for facial burns at Lankenau Hospital and released, according to a hospital spokesman.

"Our first fire fighters on the scene started to enter the building but were hit with an explosion," said Fire Commissioner Joseph Rizzo. "There are the usual supplies that these places have — propane tanks and things like that — which blow up."

However, owner Anthony L. Teti said there was no propane or other explosive material in the buildings.

Rizzo said the complex, which sprawls over half a block, was engulfed in flames when the first of 17 engine companies and five ladder companies arrived on the scene about 7:15 P.M.

He said the cause of the fire, which was brought under control at 8:54 P.M., is under investigation.

Rizzo said the evacuated families returned to their homes late last night.

"One of our main concerns was that the fire didn't spread to those homes, Rizzo said. "We had men up on the roofs."

FROM *THE BULLETIN* AND *PHILADELPHIA DAILY NEWS*

INTROSPECTION

- So, what's your self-rating on decisiveness?

- Are you a genuinely decisive person, or do you tend to stand motionless on the train platform?

- Can you easily recall an important event when you were decisive? What factor(s) drove your action?

- Can you easily recall an important event when you were indecisive? What factor(s) drove your inaction?

- Can you name one decision-making process model that you've seriously studied and really tried to use?

- Can you recall an important event when you went with your strong gut feeling—or ignored it? What was the result?

- As a leader, on a scale of 1-10, just how important is your popularity to you? Is there any chance at all that you're sacrificing some effectiveness for being popular?

CHAPTER 4

Self-Discipline

YOU MAY HAVE HAD DIFFERENT EXPERIENCES, but I've never met an outstanding leader who did not have an abundance of self-discipline. This is simply the ability to get yourself to act—regardless of your emotional state. Self-discipline is what allows a person to continuously demonstrate amazing persistence and unwavering focus.

We all have an array of the best intentions, but sometimes it's just very difficult to spring into action; and it's rarely difficult to come up with an excuse to justify why we didn't act. Remember my earlier thoughts on how easy it is to rationalize anything?

The importance of self-discipline is magnified if you are a leader. Mainly because everybody is watching your behavior; they're watching your actions all the time. I would suggest to you that self-discipline is actually a tool; an essential leadership personal development tool. Some people in leadership positions choose to use this valuable self-discipline tool; many others do not.

AN INTROSPECTION

However, all the outstanding leaders that I've known make excellent use of the tool. You see their self-discipline tool in use almost daily. The successful leaders are the ones who keep building... slowly... persistently... one event... one week at a time; all the while adding to the degree of difficulty. They use their self-discipline to just secure a beachhead; they're just trying to get a footprint, or even a toe-hold, into the land of their vision. Because, once they arrive on the beachhead, they can look back and they see all that they overcame. With greater confidence, they can now build momentum toward permanent change.

In addition to being a personal tool, self-discipline is also an incredible asset. With it, you can raise the performance level of an entire unit or organization or even make yourself into a new and better person, and therefore, a better leader.

The absolute pinnacle of self-discipline is when you reach the point that when you make a firm, conscious, well-thought-out decision—even if you don't tell anyone—it's a done deal. Your decision becomes not a matter of *if*, but *when*, because your self-discipline will force everything else to fall in line. Even if other people doubt you, you know in your heart that your decision is money in the bank. It's money already in the bank because you're going to do whatever it takes to succeed. You'll go around the wall, you'll go over the wall, or if you have to, you're strong enough, you're committed enough, you possess the self-discipline—to go *through* the wall.

It's sad that many of our leaders do not recognize the value of self-discipline, since it is so vital to a leader's success. It's vital because when you can discipline yourself to do that which is hardest, that which may appear to be out of your grasp, you gain personal access to a realm of results that are denied to everyone else.

Sure, they want it; but, they're not willing to pay that steep a price. Your willingness, your persistence, your self-discipline to go the extra mile brings you benefits that others only talk about—or dream of. Consider American author, salesman, and motivational speaker Zig Ziglar's take on going the extra mile: "There's no traffic jams out there; there's not a lot of people around you!"

It's important not to confuse the word I used earlier, *persistence*, with *stubbornness*. These are two very different concepts. When we're persistent, we understand and accept that our daily motivation can ebb and flow. We expect and are prepared for life's ups and downs. We know that every single day is not going to be filled with endless sunshine. But we also know that our persistence and self-discipline usually pay off; because if we just keep taking action day after day, we eventually and inevitably produce results.

And, through our life experiences, we know that early positive results can be very motivating. Even little victories can pump us up and keep us going. Don't we feel reinvigorated and recommitted when that first five-pound weight loss falls off from our planned diet/physical fitness program? Don't we feel that our efforts were rewarded?

However, you must be careful because stubbornness can be a very short stone's throw from persistence. Leaders must guard against stubbornness; it takes the good quality of persistence too far. When we're stubborn, we may be unduly or unwisely adamant or inflexible.

AN INTROSPECTION

Sometimes, though no one's fault, the direction of the "organizational wind" unexpectedly changes on a leader. Sadly, we see some of our leaders melt down when such change occurs, because they're way too stubbornly locked in to their initial plan or vision. The unit or organization keeps sailing along; but it's going off-course.

The truly special leaders that I've known consistently react in a positive fashion to any new wind. These are the leaders who quickly adjust the sails accordingly and keep moving forward with a revised or even brand-new plan or vision. Keep in mind that old Chinese proverb that fits so well: "If we don't change our direction, we're likely to end up where we're headed."

This leadership value of self-discipline may be the one that is most conducive to improvement a little bit at a time. Some of the other values presented here might suggest an "either-or" condition. Like honesty; most people would feel that you either are honest or you are not. You are usually not working toward becoming more honest. However, a leader's journey toward achieving total self-discipline frequently comes in smaller, progressive, positive steps. Be comfortable with that. Remain aware that one of the secrets of mastering self-discipline is to keep regularly racking up small chunks of success to be piled one on top of another.

LEADERSHIP VALUES

THE WEASEL

I have always believed that a core component of effectively drawing on your self-discipline energy stockpile is to not waste those protracted efforts. The best way to do this is to truly recognize what brings you happiness. This will help you avoid ego-driven efforts that may bring you prestige and/or rewards, but little in the way of genuine happiness. Unless you're focused on a noble cause, why even start on any arduous journey of self-discipline to achieve a goal that will not bring you satisfaction or happiness? Sometimes we receive a seemingly "wonderful opportunity" in life, but yet have the wisdom to know that it's the wrong thing for us.

Throughout my career, I was fortunate enough to have the opportunity to interview for the Deputy Fire Commissioner and/or Commissioner position, or just have it handed to me, five times. This was one of those seemingly wonderful opportunities that turned out not to be so.

A retired chief officer who was working on the transition team of Philadelphia's newly-elected mayor first approached me informally to ascertain my interest in the Deputy Commissioner (Car #2) position. I told him that while I was honored to be considered, I was not interested. Shortly after that, I received a formal offer in the form of a confidential phone call from an official member of the mayor's transition team. He invited me to sit for a promotional interview with selected members of

AN INTROSPECTION

city government, community leadership, and the transition team. I respectfully declined the offer, stating again that I had no interest in being promoted to the non-civil service position.

Several days later, while on-duty, I received a call from the mayor's office asking if I was available to meet with the mayor immediately after work. I was told to keep the meeting confidential. The caller had no interest in hearing that I had recently twice declined any possible promotion offer.

I arrived in City Hall in full dress uniform and sat anxiously in the reception area pondering how many times I had to say "No." The wait was short; the secretary led me into a large, dark-paneled, rectangular room with a classic, expensive wood desk at the far end. Waiting for me were the mayor and his chief of staff.

They came forward to greet me and we shook hands; then the mayor returned to his chair behind the desk. The chief of staff and I sat facing him across the impressive desk.

As the secretary exited toward the door, the mayor told her, "Hold all my calls."

The mayor got right to it, "So, I'm told you don't want to be considered for promotion to a deputy commissioner position in the fire department. Is that right?"

"Yes, sir. That's correct; but I do recognize and appreciate the honor of even being considered by you and your administration."

"Do you mind telling me why? From what I'm hearing, several people think that you would be a perfect fit for the position."

"I just don't want it, sir," I said, "I'm quite happy serving in my present capacity."

"Listen, Chief, this is a wonderful opportunity. I'm going to be mayor here for eight years, not four. And, I can tell you that in my time in office I will be selecting another fire commissioner. You taking this initial promotion puts you right in line for the strongest consideration for the top job when the time comes."

I replied, "I understand and I appreciate it. I'm just not interested."

The mayor paused for a few seconds and then said, "Do you see that window behind me, Chief?"

"Yes."

"Well, look out it and tell me what you see in store for the fire department."

I said two words, "Storm clouds."

The mayor smiled and nodded gently in agreement. He said, "Good. You're right. If there are no concessions from the union, the fire commissioner will have some tough decisions to make. Not just for your department, but for all of city government. We've got to get control of these expenditures. We have to make some across-the-board changes to get the City heading in the right direction."

AN INTROSPECTION

"I know, Mr. Mayor. Anyone who watches the news or reads the papers understands that some major changes are coming."

Then the mayor asked me to explain in specific terms why I was turning down this "career opportunity."

"It's not one thing, sir. It's a combination of factors. First of all, I love the fire department. I love the mission, the people, and how it makes me feel. Once you move into any of these appointed positions, it's like a clock starts ticking toward the end of your career. I've witnessed it over and over. Our brightest young stars will accept the promotion and then be out of a job each time there's a new election and the incoming administration wants to get their team in there. I have friends who are now gone from the job who tell me they wish they could turn back the clock—before their ego or other factors blinded them with more money, power, and prestige. The way I feel today about the job, I can see myself possibly staying for forty years."

The mayor countered, "That's not true; they can all return to their previous civil service position."

For the first time, the Chief of Staff spoke, "Technically, Mr. Mayor, you're right. They are entitled to do that, but few do—especially returning for any extended period."

"Okay, that's one thing. What else?"

"The storm clouds," I said, "I believe that the fire department is going to bear a significant portion of any fiscal belt-tightening you have in mind. I think we're going to go through

LEADERSHIP VALUES

another painful period of delayed recruit classes, company or station closings, and maybe even layoffs again. I've been through all that slashing, downsizing, and restructuring, and I don't want to be remembered primarily for helping to initiate those actions."

"No doubt some changes are going to be made," the mayor added, "but that's what leadership is all about. What else is preventing you from joining our team?"

"To lay it all out there, Mr. Mayor, in general, I don't like or have the emotional maturity to deal with politicians. I've been dealing with them on a regular basis for three and a half years now and I find that they're different from us. Different—and I don't mean in a good way. I find that they have different values than those of us in the fire service."

When pressed for specifics about this, I proceeded to tell the mayor of two recent political intrusions into the fire department's operations that vividly illustrated my point. I felt that both tales pointed to a clear lack of concern by city politicians for the genuine welfare of the Department and the citizens.

Slightly annoyed, the mayor said, "Well, that's not me; check with the out-going commissioner. I was always totally straight with him. You can ask him if I ever pulled anything. Go ahead, give him a call to see what he thinks."

Just then, the secretary buzzed in on the desk intercom. The mayor reminded her that he had said to hold all his calls.

AN INTROSPECTION

When he learned that a noted cleric was on the line, he said, "Excuse me, I want to take this call. Stay right here; I'll only be a minute."

As the mayor talked on the phone, I began to look around and drink in the refined environment. Turning slightly right and left, I noted the distinctive wall paintings, the expensive furniture, and the plush carpet. However, when I actually turned my body a full quarter-turn to the left I was shocked at what I saw.

Sitting on a sofa against the wall, right by a closed side door that I had passed as I approached the mayor's desk, was a thin, young man, in a gray suit. He wore dark-rimmed glasses to complement his neatly trimmed black hair. I could plainly see that he had an opened notepad in one hand and a pen in his other hand.

We locked eyes; he inhaled deeply as his face pinkened at being caught in the act. I hoped my eyes and facial expression would signal the disgust and anger that I felt quickly surging at that moment. This weasel had been instructed to stealthily slip in the side door unnoticed and quietly take a position behind me. He must have entered as the greetings and handshakes were taking place with the task of recording my statements—without my knowledge! No doubt, his spying expertise would call for him to slip out unnoticed through the same side door when the parting exchanges took place. It was only the phone call interruption allowing me to look around that exposed the treachery.

In that moment, I felt like God spoke to me, *Good move, Gary. These are not the type of people you want to be involved with.*

I felt that the interview ended with no apparent animosity. The mayor was cordial and thanked me for my "refreshing honesty." He said that I had his respect and that he looked forward to seeing me at upcoming fire department events. We shook hands and the Chief of Staff walked me to the same far door that I initially entered through.

Once again, there were only three of us in the room. The weasel was gone.

AN INTROSPECTION

Completed in 1901, Philadelphia's City Hall is the nation's largest municipal building and the tallest masonry building in the world. Chambers for the executive, legislative, and judicial branches of government are housed in almost 700 rooms. Constructed with no steel or iron framing, the brick, marble, and granite building is one of America's most honored architectural structures. It has deserved placement on the National Register of Historic Places.

INTROSPECTION

- So, how would you rate your personal level of self-discipline?

- Are you the "hang tough" type with a track record of seeing worthwhile things through to the end, even when others are jumping ship?

- Can you point to any personal or professional triumph that became a triumph only because you were persistent and went the extra mile?

- How tough are you on *yourself*? I bet some of you would find it easier to climb Mount Everest than to cut yourself some slack. I have found this to be a common trait in highly effective leaders with a strong value system.

- But, is there any point where your uncompromising quest for self-perfection can ever become counter-productive? I think the answer is a resounding "Yes." I know it can be an enormous struggle, but it's so much healthier to find a way to give yourself the same break that you're so comfortable giving to others. Try it; try being as tolerant and understanding of yourself as you are to others.

CHAPTER 5

Accountability

**ACCOUNTABILITY IS YOUR SENSE OF PERSONAL RESPON-
SIBILITY.** A problem some organizations occasionally have with its newer leaders is that, unfortunately, some of them want the money, the benefits, the prestige, and the "glory," but they won't accept their personal accountability. They don't want to be held accountable for anything. They don't have the emotional maturity—the right stuff—to be a true leader.

We've all seen these leaders; they are the ones who consistently attempt to blame others, pass the buck, and invent excuses. Is it just me that feels this way? Why is it that so many of the so-called leaders who complain the loudest about the way the ball bounces are frequently the ones who dropped it in the first place?

In some organizations today, the "Blame Game" has become part of the culture. And, sadly, some of our leaders have bought into this negative culture in which:

- Complaining is raised to an art form.
- Bad-mouthing the boss is a favorite pastime.
- Pointing fingers at others is the #1 form of organizational aerobic exercise.
- Negative "Monday morning quarterbacking" is almost at the level of a job requirement.

I suggest to you that these people who engage in these activities are not really leaders at all. They are merely "organizational employees" who have been placed in leadership positions. They're hoping to fool the top leadership team, their co-workers, their subordinates, and maybe even the public.

But how can they fool *everybody*, especially over an extended period of time? That's extremely difficult to do; some organizations have been around for a very long time and are virtually foolproof in detecting leadership imposters.

It's been my experience that if you are working in a high-quality organization as a leader, you can run from your accountability—but you can't really hide. Any successful hiding you manage to do will be relatively temporary. After all, they didn't get to be a truly high-quality organization without arming themselves with top-notch leadership up and down the line. And figuring out your act isn't going to be that great a challenge for them.

Let me be crystal clear. What all high-quality organizations expect—truly, *need*—is for their leaders to live up to not many, not most, but *all* of their responsibilities. Be accountable for every single one. If you're going to take the whole leadership paycheck, do the

AN INTROSPECTION

whole leadership job. Do it all; not just the parts that you like or that you're good at.

It's only fair that top leadership has these accountability expectations. When someone receives a promotion, in addition to the usual pay raise, he/she also gets power and legitimate authority. If used properly, that power and authority can create energy... and energy can lead to action... and action is how ideas (visions) are turned into reality.

But, don't miss the point. The reason that leaders are given more power and more authority when they get promoted is because they are given *more* responsibilities. And with increased leadership responsibility comes the dreaded "accountability factor." You are going to be held accountable to meet both the higher expectations and the higher obligations on you. Don't forget, you're being compensated to perform at the higher leadership level.

So, when you're in a leadership position, and, it doesn't really matter whether you're in sales, administration, maintenance, research, education, the arts, or public service, you cannot dismiss your leadership accountability factor. A "leader" with no accountability is no leader at all.

Have you ever watched a leader who is accused of a crime being interviewed by the news media? Sometimes, he or she stands on the courthouse steps claiming to be "fuzzy or unfamiliar" with his or her exact responsibilities. They attempt to maintain that they've been innocently caught up in a "gray area." C'mon, it is very rare that a leader will not know, or feel, what the right or ethical thing to do is.

But, if you do genuinely find yourself in that position, then your duty as a leader is still clear: find out what right is—and do that!

Most human beings (I'm not sure all) come with a "factory installed moral compass" to help keep us on the proverbial straight and narrow. Even more profound, this internal moral compass comes with alarm system wires tied directly into our brains and also into our hearts. What am I talking about? Any guesses?

Yes, our conscience.

Have you ever noticed that your conscience has two distinct and different modes of operation? In the planning or pre-event phase, when we're thinking about doing something, our conscience may be sending alarm signals to advise us: *Gary, don't do this. You know it isn't right!* Our conscience also has a post-event phase that can activate after we take an action. And this post-event phase of our conscience can judge us, sometimes very harshly.

My experience affirms my belief that good leaders leave all their conscience wires connected. Because living in today's world of free choice offers unlimited, non-stop temptations. These wise leaders appreciate the incredibly reliable guidance that our conscience can offer. Sometimes, the only single voice telling the leader the absolute, painful, real truth is the voice of his or her conscience!

AN INTROSPECTION

THE CAPTAIN WAS A CON MAN

My aide Tommy and I were walking back to our Deputy Chief's vehicle on a sundrenched, autumn Saturday afternoon. We were feeling so pleased with the outstanding firefighting efforts of our first division companies in battling a nasty all-hands fire in Chinatown. However, coming down 10th Street, I saw that the fourth-due engine company's 1500 GPM pumper was sitting in the middle of the street not connected to any hydrant.

In the PFD at that time, failure to attach a large suction hose to a hydrant was a cardinal strategic and tactical error committed by an engine company officer. Walking toward the pumper, I was certain that I would learn that the blunder was the fault of an inexperienced acting lieutenant. So, I planned to handle it as a training reminder and then move on.

However, when the pumper operator told me that the officer in charge was a second division captain from another shift who was working overtime, I had my aide summon him immediately to meet me on the corner. I had never worked directly with this officer but had some basic knowledge of his reputation. He had about twenty years on the job, and my peers felt that his performance was "Just okay, nothing special."

Because of his experience and rank, I was upset but remained in control when I sternly asked him, "Captain, what were you thinking when you disobeyed the Department's long-standing policy on obtaining an adequate water supply for the pumper? Explain your apparent terrible lack of judgment to me."

The captain took several seconds to gather his thoughts and then replied, "Chief, you're absolutely correct; it was totally my fault. I just got lazy. I know better and I accept full responsibility. I truly do understand the Department's policy and the safety implications. I do realize the critical need for me to have an adequate water supply. I apologize to you and I promise there will be no repeat behavior."

Does that sound like someone accepting his accountability? It sure did to me. I remember my surprise at his comments; no doubt, influenced by his mediocre reputation. I mumbled a few sentences and then walked away, content with the discussion's outcome. On the ride back to quarters, I told Tommy how impressed I was with the captain's reaction.

Six months later, fate brought that captain and me together again. During the yearly routine officer transfers, he was moved to my division and placed on my platoon. He would be working for me and reporting directly to one of my assigned battalion chiefs for the next three years.

At that time, every fire station had to undergo a thorough close inspection every six months by their division commander. It was a big deal; the division commander had to complete and send to Headquarters five pages of forms attesting to the

AN INTROSPECTION

company and station's readiness, cleanliness, maintenance, training, records, and much more. Because this maximum effort was only extended twice per year, captains historically spent a couple weeks (or longer) preparing for the Deputy Chief's inspection. For a commanding officer to do otherwise would be a blatant show of disrespect for their position and responsibility, the Department, and the division commander.

The captain, his battalion chief, and I all agreed upon an inspection date that was two months away. I liked providing the extra time for newly assigned captains in case any issues needed special attention. I felt that this eight-week "cushion" would result in a problem-free inspection and get our working relationship off to a good start.

On the day of the formal inspection, I was shocked at the poor condition of the station, the fire engine, and everything else. In addition to equipment being strewn haphazardly throughout the station, the fire engine compartments were dirty and contained tools that had not been cleaned from a previous fire two days before the inspection. None of the logs, journals, or important books kept on the fire engine were being updated as required. Worse; the air level on two of the breathing apparatus cylinders was low. It couldn't have been much worse if I had shown up with no warning.

After twenty disappointing minutes of walking around with the captain, I abruptly halted the inspection. I led him into the office and angrily said, "Captain, what are you doing here? You haven't shown me one thing that meets the Department's standards. What do you have to say for yourself?" Can you guess what he said?

He looked me right in the eye and said, "Chief, you're absolutely correct, it was totally my fault. I just got lazy. I know better and I accept full responsibility. I truly do understand the Department's policy on station and member readiness and cleanliness. I apologize to you and I promise there will be no repeat behavior."

Apparently, this ass had forgotten our conversation at the Chinatown fire. He was using this tactic like a "Get out of jail free" card. I wondered how many times in his sub-mediocre career had he utilized this con to shirk his duty—and his accountability.

The captain probably felt that receiving a blistering reprimand and a poor inspection grade from me were a satisfactory exchange for his eight weeks of inaction. What he *didn't* recognize was that something far more important than the chewing out or "Improvement Needed" station inspection grade had occurred because of his dereliction of duty.

Following his character-revealing reply, he lost my support, my respect, and above all—he lost my trust. Forever. And, he never knew it.

AN INTROSPECTION

That's a potential result if you're a leader who purposely and consistently chooses to act without any accountability. If you're caught, there's certainly an immediate obvious and expected public price to pay that you are able to see and experience.

However, there are also quite often unwritten, unspoken, and beneath-the-radar "costs" that you are unaware of. These silent costs (reactions) assessed by others based on your lack of integrity can be seriously damaging your reputation and career; while you mistakenly think that the momentary discomfort or embarrassment that you experience immediately after the event renders you "Paid in full."

But that's not always how it pans out. In many of these negative character-revealing moments, the offenders are just unable to clearly see the extent of the damage they've done *to themselves*.

I believe that no matter how difficult it may be for a leader to immediately accept full accountability—and modify his/her behavior, when you factor everything in, it's the much wiser path to travel.

LEADERSHIP VALUES

Accepting your accountability means that you are willing to be both responsible and answerable for your actions, decisions, and choices. Although accepting your accountability may not require you to swear a public oath, your decision nonetheless requires you to live with integrity.

PHOTO COURTESY OF THE PHILADELPHIA FIRE DEPARTMENT

INTROSPECTION

- Do you score high in the leadership accountability value?

- When something goes wrong, is your first reaction to blame others, pass the buck, or invent excuses to cover for yourself? Can you think of a time when you did this? How did it make you feel?

- Are you a leader who has no problem accepting accountability for your own actions, yet simply can't stand being responsible for those under you? What level of leadership maturity do you think this indicates?

- If someone who reports to you makes a major error, what's your procedure to *ensure* that the unacceptable behavior has been corrected?

- Do you recall any recent messages from your moral compass? Are you certain that your conscience wires are still hooked up?

CHAPTER 6

Optimism

ELLA WHEELER WILCOX (1883) WROTE, "Laugh and the whole world laughs with you. Weep and you weep alone." How true. I certainly don't want to be around people who are depressing and miserable. So, why would anybody want to be around *me* if I were in a prolonged depressed state—especially if I was their leader?

Do you know or work with someone who is the ultimate cynic, skeptic, bummer, downer, pessimist, gloom and doom, glass half-empty type? And you know that there are millions of these people out there. Sadly, we even have our share in leadership positions.

Have you ever looked into research on positive and negative energy fields? There is growing evidence that all living things give off an invisible field of energy, including you and me (Orloff, 2004). Some theories hold that our varying levels of consciousness and moods are responsible for creating these fields of energy. And if you're not aware

AN INTROSPECTION

of the concept, you can't even begin to control the energy. It just happens; we emit vibrations or auras at various intensities. But here's the important point: when we are in close proximity to one another, we all *feel*, we all pick up on, each other's human energy field. And study after study indicates that the energies can affect us both in work and at home.

The good news is that we can all control our own personal energy field to some degree. If we're aware of it, we can make a personal *choice* to be positive rather than negative in so many ways. Even when interacting with others, we can control this to some degree by opting not to pollute our personal energy field with downers, nitwits, and bummers.

Try this experiment in the upcoming weeks. At home, and especially at work, start noticing everybody's personal energy field. Is anybody consistently bringing you down? I'm not talking about someone having a bad day or a co-worker going through a rough stretch. I mean day in and day out, 52 weeks a year, nothing but 100 percent negativity!

There's potential good news. In some cases, you may be able to reduce the contamination level that you receive from these people. My dear friend Ted Bateman, who has served in various public safety roles for several decades, has a unique approach. He always makes it a point to very quickly identify consistently negative people—and then he goes to great lengths to reduce their influence on him. How? Ted does this by applying his fire department hazardous materials background; specifically, taking the approach that first responders would when dealing with a radiation leak. He treats these negative people like they are radioactive isotopes.

A widely accepted three-step emergency response approach to mitigating radioactive incidents is based on time, distance, and shielding. So, to the degree possible, Ted will consciously (1) **limit the time** he spends in the company of these negative people. If he can, he will (2) **physically keep his distance** from their negative energy fields whether in an office, in a meeting, or even at a social event. And, he will effectively (3) **shield himself** from the contamination of their endless negative words, thoughts, and outlook by utilizing his staff, other people, and/or creative physical configurations.

Ted takes this approach because after a few years, he just got tired of processing all the negativity. He found it time-consuming and depleting on *his* personal energy level. Fortunately, many years ago, for my own mental health, I successfully copied his behavior and significantly freed myself from the anchor of others' negativity.

So, how important is it for a leader to have a sense of humor; to actually smile or even laugh once in a while? It's essential. Laughter has incredible positive power for all of us, including the leader. Studies have actually shown that a positive physical effect occurs when we laugh; we produce peptides and endorphins. Did you know that it's a scientific fact that tears of happiness have a different chemical composition than tears of sadness? (Fisher, 2014). To laugh is a natural human instinct. So why do so many of today's leaders actively suppress the instinct?

AN INTROSPECTION

Becoming the leader does not mean you have to be 100 percent serious about every single micro-issue under the sun. Yes, you should absolutely take your job and especially your responsibilities seriously; but, try to take *yourself* a little less seriously.

It's no secret that people want to follow someone who is optimistic, not pessimistic. Optimists habitually, or in a particular event, anticipate and expect a favorable outcome. They simply believe that it's going to work out: "Hey guys, even though it may look bleak today... eventually we'll get through this... I know we're gonna be alright."

However, in so many organizations today, a major challenge for the leaders is just to stay strong, not to get worn down—just survive. But, sadly, many of our really good leaders do get worn down. They get beat up and done in by the nay-sayers, fault-finders, and the small-thinkers. And in some organizations, the pessimists far out-number the optimists.

So, as a leader, this is why you must be mentally and emotionally strong enough not to let negative people easily shake you from your core values, beliefs, goals, and vision.

I believe that top-level leaders should regularly make the time to thank all fellow leaders who serve with and below them who unashamedly "wear" their optimism on their sleeve. These optimistic leaders are the ones fighting that front-line battle against organizational negativity. They recognize the potential destructive force of continuous pessimism and they battle against it wherever and whenever they encounter it. It's not easy to continually stand firmly against ceaseless negativity. So, appreciate and value these special leaders; recognize the enormous organizational benefits that their unwavering optimism brings.

And in difficult times, remember this relevant quote from Albert Einstein on leaders getting worn down: "Great spirits have always encountered violent opposition from mediocre minds."

"THERE WON'T EVEN BE ENOUGH LEFT OF US TO BURY"

Very early in my position as a deputy chief, I learned that *pretending* to be optimistic can sometimes be just as vital to team effectiveness as true optimism.

At 94°F, it was one of those brutally hot, muggy Sunday afternoons in August when the Fire Communications Center (FCC) received a call from Police Radio that "an explosion" had occurred somewhere in the area of Atlantic Richfield Company Refinery's (ARCO) North Yard. Within seconds, phone calls started pouring in to the FCC describing a thunderous explosion. "I think a plane just crashed," said one caller. Another said, "There must be a wicked multi-car crash on the expressway." The main problem for the FCC was that no caller could provide a specific location for "the explosion."

I had heard the explosion myself while talking with Battalion Chief Harry Cusick in First Division Headquarters.

AN INTROSPECTION

We both hustled to the window of the office and looked south toward the two large nearby refineries we protected. We saw nothing.

Harry said, "This can't be good, Chief. I'm heading down that way—just in case."

Two minutes later, at 1:48 PM, the FCC transmitted the signal for Box #5146, 32nd and Maiden Lane and attached the Hazardous Materials Task Force to the responding units.

There were very few initial box transmissions that drew the immediate attention of every on-duty Philadelphia Firefighter like the refinery boxes. No matter what rank you held or where you were stationed, when a refinery box number was transmitted, you stopped what you were doing and listened for the report of the first arriving unit. These specific box numbers were seared into the consciousness of nearly all our firefighters due to the continuous epic battles we fought there—and the men we lost battling those fires. Just eight years earlier, at the Gulf Refinery, eight of our brothers were killed in a single fire. There were never going to be any false alarms on a refinery box number, because the box was only struck upon notification from the refinery switchboard that their fire brigade could not handle a situation.

Harry and his first battalion aide arrived even before the first-due engine company. He reported a high-pressure gas leak coming from one of the butane storage tanks in ARCO's

LEADERSHIP VALUES

North Yard. This section of the refinery was a mere 200 feet from the Schuylkill Expressway, one of the city's main traffic thoroughfares. There was no visible fire and no sphere's sprinkler system had activated—something that would pinpoint the exact problem unit. As Harry gave his report over the fire radio band, we all heard a thunderous roar in the background. At 1:52 PM, I was dispatched along with a medic unit.

This section of the North Yard held four 10,000-barrel spherical pressure tanks containing liquid butane; one barrel contains 42 gallons. Each tank had a diameter of 43 feet and was several stories in height. In short: these were enormous tanks! And it was a true worst-case scenario because a five to eight mile per hour wind was pushing the flammable vapors directly across the Schuylkill Expressway toward the Tasker Homes, a low-income housing project in South Philly.

I knew from studying and attending seminars that I was on the scene and in command of a potentially catastrophic event for the City. If a liquefied petroleum gas (LPG) tank this size was to blow, it could leave hundreds of people dead and burned and blocks of scorched earth surrounding a football-field-sized crater. It had happened in other places.

The ARCO fire brigade determined that the ten-inch vacuum breaker seal on tank "RM–40" had failed. The liquid butane, under roaring pressure, was escaping into the atmosphere and quickly turning into a gas. A distinct white cloud was rolling

AN INTROSPECTION

down the sides of the tank and drifting through the property line's chain link fence onto the expressway. Vehicles with red-hot mufflers and an occasional back-fire were passing right through the vapor cloud which never rose above two feet off the ground. To try to dissipate the heavier than air vapors, ARCO's fire brigade manually activated the tank's water sprays and turned on several fixed water spray monitors. Their efforts were overwhelmed by the volume of the gas.

At that time, Chief Cusick was the PFD's premier hazardous materials expert. How fortunate I was to have him with me. I quickly ran my strategy by him and he concurred with everything. Normally a happy-go-lucky guy with an ever-present smile, I could see the deep concern all over his face. The more you knew about LPG explosions, the more you *should* have been concerned—and Harry knew an awful lot.

I was probably even more concerned than he was, but I managed to calmly say, "We'll be alright, Har'; I know we're gonna get through this okay." I think he believed me. More importantly, I don't think that he detected that I was scared shitless inside.

The strategy was to let the ARCO personnel focus primarily on shutting down the leak. The PFD's most urgent priorities were to stop traffic on the Schuylkill Expressway, evacuate the first two streets inside the Tasker Homes, eliminate all sources of ignition, set up unmanned water cannons with spray patterns to absorb the butane vapors, and keep taking meter readings to stay abreast of the vapor travel and danger zones. I requested a second alarm and asked the FCC to have a high-ranking police supervisor contact me to expedite the evacuation of the project homes.

I instructed all four of the incoming first-alarm engine companies to work together as one large single team in getting the four deluge guns set up. That way, the first master stream devices would come on line much quicker and we could retreat to a safer, vapor-free position that much sooner.

As the firefighters were setting up the first deluge guns, I stood alone save for Petey, my trusty division aide, in the middle of the now traffic-free expressway. Looking down, we could see the undulating butane vapors slowly gliding over and past our boots and gently flowing toward the projects.

It was heart-pounding to be standing in the middle of the vapor cloud wondering if your next breath would be your last. But what was the alternative? This was one of those rare moments that drove home the true implications of our oath of office.

I must have turned away from the leaking tank and looked back at the projects a dozen times when Petey asked me, "Chief, why do you keep looking behind us?"

AN INTROSPECTION

"Because there are no sources of ignition right here, Pete. If ignition comes, the flame is going to start in the projects behind us and follow the vapors right back into the tank."

"That's good then, right? We'll see it start and we can outrun it," he replied.

"Outrun the flame spread? Are you serious? LPG flame travels at fifteen feet per second—and we've got full bunker gear on. If the vapors are in the flammable range, all it will take is one spark in that project; a refrigerator motor kicking on, an activated light switch. Anything! If that tank explodes, there won't even be enough left of us to bury."

I could see instantly that I upset him. I recovered and said, "But, don't worry about it. I've had several of these jobs before and they all worked out. We're all going to be fine; nobody is dying here today. Okay?"

With my optimism, I saw the color begin to return to his face. Sure, I had lied; I had never handled anything so potentially catastrophic. But Petey bought my optimism and returned immediately to function as his old reliable self.

One by one, the members brought eight deluge guns on line with breathtaking speed and we formed a semi-circle discharging a huge, overlapping water curtain. Thankfully, the wind direction never changed significantly and the vapors passed through and got absorbed in our curvature of water spray.

LEADERSHIP VALUES

I knew that any optimism or encouragement that I displayed via radio transmissions from the relative safety of a distant designated command post location would have diminished value. If my optimism were to have any meaningful effect, it demanded a face-to-face delivery. So, while the companies were setting up, I stayed right there with them, moving amid the vapor cloud and the deafening noise of the pressure relief valve, providing loud encouragement and appreciation for all their actions. I guess I was acting a bit like a cheerleader; but I felt it was important for our success to display the optimism and confidence that would allow everyone to focus solely on their tasks at hand —and not dwell on the potential detonation.

Finally, at 8:24 PM, a two-man ARCO team, equipped with little more than breathing apparatus and some hand tools, succeeded in closing the gate valve. Six hours and thirty-six minutes of an extraordinary team effort was finally over. For much of that time, only the slenderest of threads stood between us and death. The actions of the firefighters, ARCO crews, Philadelphia Police, Housing Police, Philadelphia Gas Works, and Electric Company crews were nothing short of heroic throughout the entire ordeal.

That butane leak experience became a watershed event in my leadership development. My everlasting take-away reconfirmed that optimism must be an essential ingredient to good leadership. The worse conditions are for your team, the more

AN INTROSPECTION

important it will be for your personal optimism to be on full display—even if you're just faking it.

---

350 Flee Butane Leak
Blast Danger at ARCO Shuts Expressway
Gas Volcano Sends S. Phila. Fleeing
Gas Leak Shuts Schuylkill

Butane leak forces evacuation
Expressway near Arco closed for seven hours

Butane vapors force hundreds to evacuate
'Invisible Bomb'

FROM *THE BULLETIN, PHILADELPHIA DAILY NEWS,* AND *THE PHILADELPHIA INQUIRER*

INTROSPECTION

- Do you score high in being an optimistic person?

- Are you a glass half-full person? Are you sure? Would those around you agree?

- Are any negative energy fields contaminating you at work? Did I describe anybody who you work with or socialize with, whose relentless negativity just wears you down? Can you do anything about it?

- Take a moment and think of the two very best all-around leaders you ever knew; exceptional leaders who are/were "the total package." Would you say they are/were optimists or pessimists? What does your answer tell us? How important is the value of optimism to leadership?

- Is your organization primarily controlled by "Great Spirits" or "Mediocre Minds?"

CHAPTER 7

Courage

IN MY EXPERIENCE, COURAGE IS THAT QUALITY OF THE MIND that enables one to meet danger and difficulties head on—with spirit, firmness, resolution, and tenacity. This definition's reference to meeting "difficulties" is a crucial point, because chasing down an armed suspect, tending to a patient in a volatile drug-house, or crawling down a burning hallway do not have a monopoly on courage. I've found that courage takes many forms. The courage required for a leader to make a tough decision can be just as frightening for some as kicking in a door to serve a warrant.

Our best leaders display an all-encompassing type of courage that has them standing tall all the time, not just during formally declared "emergencies." Exemplary leaders show courage routinely in the office, the board room, the court room, the laboratory, the warehouse, at staff meetings, in social settings, and everywhere else that leadership is expected.

Sometimes, leaders need courage for even the simplest of acts; for example, uttering those sometimes painful or embarrassing words, "I don't know." Some are so scared that they simply don't do it. When you're a leader, admitting that you don't know something can be an agonizing moment. After all, *you're* the leader; most people think that you're supposed to know.

Have you ever had one of those uncomfortable moments when someone asks you a question and every fiber in your body is urging you to "dance" on the issue? I've seen so-called leaders who were so good at dancing, they should have been working at Arthur Murray Dance Studios.

But good leaders don't really need dancing skills. Sometimes, a leader's honest acknowledgement of "I don't know" can be the most courageous thing you do all month. Of course, the obligation then is that you will find out the correct answer and take the required action. Credible leaders are never afraid to say, "I don't know."

Here's another courageous leadership phrase that you may never have heard from a particular boss, or personally uttered: "I'm sorry; I apologize." Some leaders act like their promotion and their newly acquired additional responsibility and accompanying pressure excuses them from such pedestrian acts. Some people even believe that apologizing is just a sign of character weakness.

That's not the way I see it. I believe that each promotion should propel you to an even higher standard of personal conduct. Each elevation

AN INTROSPECTION

in leadership responsibility calls for you to be more mature, more developed, and more human.

Have you ever witnessed a leader attempting to apologize who just made the situation worse? He or she either doesn't care or was absent for the "Apologizing Guidelines Course." These imitation leaders' vague, insincere, poorly-timed, alibi-coated efforts, sometimes delivered via a third party, have little value.

It can require significant courage for a leader to apologize to someone. Firstly, because you're supposed to make amends or repair the damage if possible. In fact, if you're not clear on the resolution, you're supposed to ask, "What can I do to make this right?" This is where the courage comes in: by being willing to listen to the answer and then take the corrective action. And sometimes the answer may leave you weak in the knees.

Secondly, apologizing can open an emotional "door" that allows fury and anger to come rushing out at you. Courage might be needed to withstand the heat; but that's part of the apology deal.

Thirdly, offering a sincere apology implies that you're going to do your best to learn and grow from the incident. So, therefore—you can't do it again! If necessary, do you have the courage to live with this permanent behavior modification?

My definition of courage also requires meeting the issue head on. Unfortunately, courage doesn't come with any adjustable time frames. Sometimes you'll need it instantaneously; you see it, and you react. Other times, you'll see the need for courage building. The "collision" is a week or even a month out. But, you know there's some challenging situation or person out there—and it, or he/she, isn't going away. As a leader, you're just going to have to face it. But, I'll tell you this: the trick *is* in the timing. It's very difficult to be courageous when the real need has passed.

The definition also states that courage is a quality *of the mind*. You don't have to be a doctor to realize that the heart can't think, no matter how often we admiringly refer to a person's "heart." The heart is only a muscle. Therefore, courage must be a *state of mind* for any leader; an ever-present part of your individual conscience, an important piece of who you are as a leader.

There can be no continual switching of a courage reservoir "On/Off" button. Permanently throwing that switch is supposed to come with your leadership promotion. But, it's not an automatic activation: *you* must turn it "On." And you must keep it "On" permanently. As the leader, when a storm blows in, you better be at the helm of your particular ship because that's where everybody will be looking for you. A true leader always takes a totally visible position out in front. Any unexplained or unapproved absence by you during a storm will be conspicuous—and not easily forgotten.

As a leader, you'll find that you can't fool your co-workers, bosses, or especially your subordinates for too long when it comes to courage. Leadership challenges inevitably come up. It only takes a few events in which you clearly demonstrate a lack of courage for everyone to see through you like a pane of glass.

I have been associated with many truly courageous people in my time in public safety. From them, I've learned that courage need not

AN INTROSPECTION

be loud; it is often quiet. It does not require witnesses for any type of validation; many heroic acts and courageous decisions and commitments are made in solitude. And real courage, the genuine article, needs no publicity; it always speaks for itself.

I believe as well that intelligence is part of some type of a "Courageous Behavior Equation." How big a part? I don't really know... 5%?... 2%?... just ¼ of 1%? Whatever the percentage, being smart can be an essential element in an ideal courage equation.

Are you familiar with the noted educator and writer Jonathan Kozol? He takes my point further by advising us to "Pick battles big enough to matter and small enough to win." What's he saying? As a leader, you can't be revving up your "personal war machine" every time something doesn't go your way. Over the long run, the odds are against you; you just can't win every single time. Some issues, some battles, simply aren't worth your effort. So, save your energy for the truly *meaningful* battles. And you know there will be more than enough of them.

In "small enough to win," Kozol also prompts the question: When you're facing an absolute, guaranteed, losing battle, how smart is it for the leader to take it on? Maybe, as the leader you need to seriously consider a non-confrontational option. Or perhaps, the smartest choice is to take no action at all; just bide your time. Otherwise, with defeat inevitable, you may simply be wasting your time, energy, and precious resources. When you choose to enter a battle as a leader, you often take your "troops" right along with you. And most times, they didn't even get a vote. Remember: leadership is rarely just about you.

LEADERSHIP VALUES

My final thoughts on "charging the hill under heavy fire" courage: I understand the concept that people can display both what is referred to by the "experts" as "Smart Courage" or "Stupid Courage." And, I agree that smart courage is always infused and bolstered with intelligence, self-discipline, focus, skill, and morals; it's pretty easy to see smart courage in action. I also accept that stupid courage needs only audacity and that it too is usually easy to recognize.

But I must tell you that on many occasions I have witnessed a person exhibiting stupid courage—and I usually respected it—and sometimes loved it! To witness another human being acting in a bold, daring, fearless, "To Hell with it!" manner, can occasionally leave you impressed, effected, and even breathless. Not being able to walk in the shoes of these intrepid persons at their critical moment of decision, I have now grown reluctant to judge them, especially in any negative light. How can I know *all* that was in their mind or their heart when they charged that hill? Maybe the leadership book theorists need a better word than "stupid"; maybe it's only stupid *to them*. Maybe we have to become a little slower to criticize when someone's concept of courage doesn't match ours.

Finally, to truly understand the value of courage, I believe that you must examine its connection to the concept of failure. Some people have no idea how strong our human fear of failure is. The fear is so incredibly strong that it can overcome how humans are programmed and override our innate nature.

Our nature as infants and children is to take chances and risks, to learn and grow from early mistakes. That's the way we're all born.

AN INTROSPECTION

Just consider a child learning to walk. Why doesn't the child just give up after falling several hundred or even several thousand times? The child doesn't give up because children are fear**less**. Small children don't understand failure; they have to be taught the concept. So, as we grow up, most of us learn fear of failure from other people.

We imagine this strong reason for not acting. Heaven forbid, we could be labeled a "failure." We come to believe and accept this artificial judgment from other people—who are sometimes morons—of a terrible thing called failure. We can become afraid or even frozen. Because we're afraid to try because we *might* fail, many people, including some in leadership positions, spend their entire careers *and lives* sitting in a distant bleacher seat, watching the real game unfold on the field.

I believe that to really grow and become a special leader, it helps to make a personal attitude shift by reexamining how you think about failure. Some of the things and people that we label "failures" may not be so at all, because "failing" is frequently just someone's judgment. It's a word or a label that we humans place on an action, or worse, attach to a person. However, it's often a judgement that's biased, uninformed, malicious, and/or totally incorrect.

When you're a leader, you eventually must stop worrying about what other people will think or say about you—or your failures. Stop believing that there is nothing worse than being called a failure. I've learned that much of leadership (and life!) is about seizing the moment and just going for it. It really is about just getting up off your butt and doing it. Do you recall Wayne Gretsky's guarantee? "You're going to miss 100% of the shots...that you never take!"

So, demonstrate your personal positive value of *decisiveness*, and stop making excuses Throw your courage switch to the full "On" position. Get your mitt, put your jersey on, and c'mon down from the bleachers... and set a few of your great ideas in motion.

THE AROMA OF MARINARA

Believe it or not, two of my greatest leadership "lessons learned" occurred the same night—and amazingly, it was just my second shift as a brand-new lieutenant.

When I was promoted to lieutenant in the Philadelphia Fire Department, it was the policy of Headquarters to assign all newly promoted lieutenants to a different platoon and to a different division than which they previously worked. They had a long-standing preference for the sink-or-swim results that the stressful procedure placed on their newest leaders. It was truly frightening; you were working in a vastly different role, in a completely different section of the city, on a platoon where you usually knew no one, and facing unfamiliar operational challenges that you only studied (e.g. row-house fires vs waterfront fires; high-rise fires vs factory fires)—not experienced firsthand.

The way my specific schedule fell after promotion day, I was to work two 14-hour night tours and then start my regular

AN INTROSPECTION

platoon days off. My pool assignment called for me to work the first night at Engine 13 and the second night at Engine 31. Both companies were in North Philly and far from my West Philly "home." I had never even seen the two fire stations.

My first leadership lesson centers around the daily PFD officer duty of conducting a "station exercise." These were mandated one-hour events in which the officer(s) had to lead in-station training for all the on-duty firefighters. The station exercise topic list was published one month in advance, so the identical training occurred every day and every night virtually simultaneously throughout the City's fire stations.

Back then, holding the scheduled station exercise was a very big deal. Headquarters insisted that it be done, and the commissioner was maniacal in his commitment to enforcing it. You also knew that the visiting battalion chief was probably going to check on you to make sure you were fulfilling your responsibility. To choose not to hold a station exercise and risk some form of disciplinary action was a daring move for any officer, although a few did and were popular with the firefighters because of it.

My first night at Engine 13, we were dispatched to a large dumpster fire thirty minutes prior to the scheduled station exercise time and didn't return to the station for almost two hours. I legitimately missed presenting my first training exercise.

The second night was much different. At the 6 PM roll call, I made a few minor announcements and gave out the assignments to my crew. At that time in PFD history, Engine 31 was *the* busiest engine company in the city. They were one of several two-piece high-pressure engine companies (Yes, they ran with *two* 750 GPM pumpers) and were legendary both for their assigned "characters" and their firefighting bravado.

Even though I had my own fine firefighting pedigree coming from West Philly's 11th Battalion, I felt intimidated standing at roll call in front of the six firefighters. Every one of them was older than me, and half of them had spent more time firefighting than I had years on earth. They were in various states of tattered uniforms with bodies full of scars and tattoos. Most of them were severely in need of a dental plan. Half were combat war veterans, one from WWII and two from Korea. I had never seen a more hard-core looking crew... and they did nothing to make me feel welcome.

After roll call, I immediately proceeded to the second-floor office to complete the initial shift paperwork and check what station exercise I was to give that night. *Oh my, this is perfect,* I lamented. The scheduled exercise was to be held on the Scott Air Pak and I knew that all these guys would rather take a beating than don a breathing apparatus. And, *I* was going to have to spend from 7 PM to 8 PM at the head of the kitchen table lecturing them on how it works and why they needed it. I was dreading it.

As I read over the training manual, around 6:30 things got worse. I caught the aroma of fresh marinara rising from the

AN INTROSPECTION

kitchen. *Oh no; they're getting ready to sit down to a spaghetti meal shortly. How's this going to work for me?*

I came up with a "plan." I sat at the office desk—and prayed for a run. I was consumed with fear. How was I going to summon the courage to walk down those stairs...have the man on watch "hit the bells" to assemble the crew...then walk into the kitchen...request that the spaghetti and gravy pots be turned off...and announce that I was going to conduct the mandated training exercise? You might be smiling; but I bet at least someone reading this has experienced a similar near-paralyzing fear.

Somehow, at 6:59 PM, I found myself descending the old wooden stairs with our Training Manual in hand and my heart rate approaching tachycardia. With a squeaky voice, trembling knees, and probably, dilated pupils, I lectured for about forty minutes. The crew just sat around the kitchen table staring at me; they never spoke as they watched my sweat glands kick into overdrive as my internal temperature soared. It had to be *the* worst training session ever delivered that year by *any* PFD officer. That didn't matter to me though; I got through it.

So, what was the valuable leadership lesson that I learned from this experience that stuck with me forever? Namely this: that the need for my courage is (usually) going to peak at that **first** event opportunity.

No matter where I went after that, my anxiety, apprehension, or fear for conducting a station exercise in unknown and potentially "hostile territory" never rose to that level again. I learned that once you overcome your initial fear on an issue, it gets easier the second time. And, easier yet the third, and so on.

Pretty soon, courage just becomes a habit. That habit is what you do; that *habit is who you are.* You just have to always measure up that initial time. And you know that some issues are not as simple as conducting a routine training exercise. For some issues, the stakes are momentous—and the leader will **never** get another opportunity to conquer *that* particular moment.

NOTE: The second enduring leadership lesson that I learned that very night is revealed in the final chapter on Enlightenment. It's the story of a firebombing and what happened to me while commanding my first "good job" as an officer.

AN INTROSPECTION

Courage must be a state of mind.

FIRE DEPARTMENT CADETS ATTACKING A PETROLEUM PIT FIRE.

LEADERSHIP VALUES

CADETS TRAINING WITH SCALING LADDERS

PHOTOS COURTESY OF THE PHILADELPHIA FIRE DEPARTMENT

INTROSPECTION

- How would you rate your personal courage level?

- Does your courage reservoir button remain locked in the "On" position?

AN INTROSPECTION

- Are you fully comfortable saying "I don't know," or do you ever dance? In your opinion, is it really very difficult for the subordinates to detect when a leader is dancing?

- When was the last time you apologized to someone? Could it have gone better? Do you owe anyone an overdue apology right now? What's stopping you?

- Have you been recently sidestepping or avoiding some challenging situation or person out there that you know isn't going away? Is it time to display the required courage?

- Take a deeper, more personal look at Kozol's advice on picking your battles correctly. He advises us to "Select those battles that are big enough to matter...and those small enough to win." Do you believe that Kozol's advice is the absolute 100% final word on "going to war"? Or, can there *ever* be a time, for you professionally or personally, where your feelings on the issue—your personal values—simply outweigh any possible negative consequences?

CHAPTER 8

Honesty

AN IMPORTANT ASPECT OF HONESTY IS TRUTHFULNESS; it's an essential trait that all honorable people must have. One challenge to living a life in which we consistently act with total honesty is that we're all human—and therefore imperfect. It's difficult to sail through adult life without ever telling a lie.

And, there are so many kinds of lies. On occasion, some among us might lie to:
- Protect ourselves.
- Protect our privacy.
- Keep a secret.
- Enhance our image.
- Avoid embarrassment.
- Dramatize our position.
- Embellish a story.
- Just plain purposely deceive someone.

AN INTROSPECTION

We sometimes tell white lies for the sake of others; to spare someone's feelings or to lift another person's spirits. This too is human nature.

However, I have come to believe that the *most* dangerous lies we tell are not the ones to your co-workers, boss, or to your special person; they are the lies that you tell yourself. Why? Because these particular lies can actually distort your view of reality. After enough time and enough repetition, you can actually come to believe your own lies. And worse yet—act on them!

Lies have a way of getting away from us and causing tremendous, long-lasting pain and sorrow. And they can cause much more pain and sorrow if they are spoken from a leadership position. Why? Because usually more people are listening to a leader's words; therefore, more people can be hurt.

Here's the bottom line on lies: they destroy trust. And our society is built upon *mutual* trust; trust between nations, trust between organizations, trust between individual leaders, and the essential trust between a leader and his/her followers. If you think I'm overstating the importance of honesty to a leader, note the research findings of Kouzes and Pozner (2011): since 1980, honesty has been ranked the *most* important leadership attribute in admired leaders.

As a leader, one might fall down occasionally in judgment and survive completely, maybe even go on to flourish. But to miss the mark or fail in the honesty value destroys any leadership potential that a person does have because **lying makes trust impossible.** And you can't really lead without people's trust in you.

LEADERSHIP VALUES

I have one last point to make on the value of honesty. Early in my twenty-five years as a deputy chief, I spent a lengthy tour-of-duty as the PFD's Executive Officer. I reported directly to the Fire Commissioner and handled a wide variety of important special projects and all major disciplinary cases.

During these years, I had extensive interaction with persons and organizations completely outside of the Fire Service realm. It was an eye-opening experience dealing with so many who had nothing in common with our traditional departmental values which were centered around service and dedication. On a weekly and sometimes daily basis, my varied duties led me to deal with special interest groups, government agencies, politicians, attorneys, salespeople, consultants, and the media. My painful but valuable experience with these individuals and groups demonstrated to me that it is getting more challenging to identify *real* truths anymore.

The leadership lesson that I learned is that in recent years, a new, slick group has emerged who can effortlessly modify any truth through clever language or manipulation of words. These people are highly skilled practitioners whose impact and influence should never be underestimated; they can be a serious threat to anyone's leadership abilities.

You are probably familiar with their apt description: they are called "spin doctors" or "spinmeisters." Their primary mission is to have *you* act based on *their* slant on the truth. They are also talented

AN INTROSPECTION

enough to take any truth and reframe it or modify it to reduce its negative impact on themselves or those they serve.

This is not intended to alarm you, but rather to simply raise your awareness level of the existence of spin doctors and their potential damaging interaction with you and your organization. As a leader, it can be extremely risky, unwise, and naïve to conduct your business on the assumption that everyone is as honest as you.

Recognizing and successfully dealing with spin doctors is now an essential leadership skill, especially at the higher organizational levels where you interact regularly with special interest groups, government agencies, politicians, attorneys, salespeople, consultants, and the media.

My early naivete taught me to place myself on "red alert" when dealing with anyone representing an organization's advertising, sales, communications, or public relations division. I also discovered that some aides or assistants to political figures tend to employ manipulative, deceptive, and/or disingenuous tactics to attempt to get you to interpret an event from their particular perspective.

Detecting spin doctors can be a challenge to any leader primarily because these people are not going to identify their true motives during an encounter. You won't hear: *"Hi, I'm Joe Smith. I'm a world-class spin doctor and I'm here to seriously complicate your values, vision, and goals. Believe me, I can confuse you because my words are ambiguous, my facts are selective, my euphemisms are masterful, I champion unproven truths, and I can magically skirt any issue that you bring up."*

LEADERSHIP VALUES

When I first became a leader, a lot of old-timers advised me: "Keep your eyes wide open, kid." It took quite a while for me to learn that effective leadership demands keeping your *ears* just as wide open as your eyes. In my Executive Officer role, I had to quickly learn some of the tactics to look for in identifying spin doctors.

Can you easily spot them? Are you adept at quickly recognizing a spin doctor's:

- Non-denial denial?
- Non-apology apology?
- Cherry-picking of facts?
- Clever use of semantics?
- Turning attention to someone else?
- Non-direct references (e.g. "Mistakes were made.")?
- Faking insult to divert or postpone a direct reply?

Once I raised my awareness and detection levels, I was better able to spot the spin doctors. Through my efforts to rapidly identify dishonest behavior, both I and the Philadelphia Fire Department were better off.

My best advice for today's leaders is twofold. First of all, recognize that spin doctors exist all around us—and that they are just as talented and dedicated to their mission as you are to yours. Secondly, protect yourself against their danger by taking the time to study and learn their strategies, tactics, methods, and schemes.

AN INTROSPECTION

THREE LITTLE BUTTONS

While serving at the Fire Academy, I was fortunate to be quartered in the same building with the Department's Hazardous Materials Administrative Unit (HMAU). At that time, HMAU was led by Battalion Chief Bob Marchisello, an exemplary leader who had raised the level of PFD hazardous materials response to national prominence.

Like me, Bob was frequently bombarded by salespersons peddling the latest invention to allegedly make the lives of emergency responders safer and easier. After relentless mailings, telephone calls, and the application of some third-party pressure, Bob agreed to observe a demonstration of a new type of Mass Spectrometer/Gas Chromatograph.

The manufacturer claimed that the equipment came with break-through technology that would identify unknown gaseous hazardous materials more quickly and with greater accuracy than anything currently on the market. However, the focus of the marketing strategy was aimed at the unit's ease of operation. Both the literature and the manufacturer's representative himself claimed that the unit had only three buttons on the control panel and was "very simple to use." Bob invited me to attend the scheduled demonstration in his office.

After a brief pitch covering the unit's diagnostic capabilities, the company's representative launched into a ten-minute spiel repeatedly emphasizing the benefits of only having to press "these three little buttons" to immediately discover the true composition of any unknown chemical. Three little buttons: what could be simpler?

The pitch to Bob was smooth and tinged with a slight sense of urgency: "Chief, if you buy today, we'll give you 15% off our already rock-bottom price. But, the deal is only good for today. If you buy two units today, my company has authorized me to reduce the price by 25%. This is a tremendous offer for your department; but, it's only a one-time offer. Naturally, Chief, if you take advantage of today's very generous offer, we'll include free shipping."

All eyes turned toward Chief Marchisello. The sales rep was the only one in the room who didn't realize that Bob was born and raised in South Philly—where they spot guys like this from a mile away.

Bob surprised all of us when he reached into his desk drawer and pulled out a small vile of liquid (diesel fuel) and said, "Test this right now and tell us what it is. Show us how the three little buttons work."

The salesperson coughed, sputtered, and walked sheepishly to the table where his travel carriers were. He removed an expensive laptop computer from his briefcase and then proceeded to connect it to the "heavily discounted" contraption. So much for "just three little buttons"!

AN INTROSPECTION

I watched Bob rise to his feet and then square himself directly in front of the salesperson. Looking dead into the salesperson's darting eyes, Bob said, "Three buttons? Really? Are you kidding me?" The demonstration was over.

Not wanting to laugh at the guy, I left the room immediately. Only moments later, I spotted him from my office window getting into his vehicle. He had that sad, defeated "no sale" look—another spin doctor had been exposed.

THROUGH CONSTANT CLASSROOM AND HANDS-ON TRAINING AND EDUCATION, MEMBERS OF THE PFD HAZARDOUS MATERIALS TASK FORCE ARE FULLY PREPARED TO HANDLE EMERGENCIES.

PHOTO COURTESY OF THE PHILADELPHIA FIRE DEPARTMENT

LEADERSHIP VALUES

INTROSPECTION

- Do you score in the very highest percentile in honesty? As you know, in evaluating this particular value, even a score of "85" can be a huge problem.

- Examining those (rare?) occasions in which you are untruthful, can you identify a common theme to your lies? Are your lies usually to save face? To make yourself look better? To harm someone you dislike?

- Have you ever been in a situation where it didn't seem like a wise idea to volunteer the truth, so instead, you said nothing? Does that occur frequently for you? Why?

- Do you feel that keeping silent on an issue is the same thing as lying?

- Do you have sufficient skills to identify and successfully deal with spin doctors?

CHAPTER 9

Trustworthiness

THERE IS NO BETTER VALUE WITH WHICH TO FOLLOW UP HONESTY THAN TRUSTWORTHINESS. It is incredibly important to any leader, at any level. A leader must be *worthy* of trust; trust from above, from below, and peer-to-peer.

Honesty and trustworthiness are interrelated in many ways, yet there are clear distinctions. Honesty is a person's relationship to truth and morality. Trustworthiness has more to do with *relationships* between people because it indicates the degree to which one is responsible and reliable. A person can be honest with information and opinions, yet untrustworthy in his/her follow-through on promises, obligations, or duty.

If I planned to commit a crime, I might tell a friend who I considered to be trustworthy but lacking in the value of honesty. However, I would never tell a friend who was honest.

LEADERSHIP VALUES

What's the bottom line for leadership? You must possess both qualities—in abundance.

Warren Bennis, an international theorist on leadership, says, "The number one requirement of leadership is to generate and sustain trust." He rates it at the very top of the scale. Think about that: here is a person with extraordinary leadership credentials himself, saying that there is nothing more valuable to a leader than trustworthiness.

Whatever their organization, most employees throw trust around with the same frequency as they toss around manhole covers—which is exactly why trust is so priceless *if* the leader has it. It's important because trust is the "emotional glue" that binds the followers and the leader together (Bennis and Nanus, 1985).

Do you want an assessment tool to evaluate *your* leadership effectiveness? How about this? The accumulation of trust, how much trust you are awarded by your subordinates is one very accurate and significant measure of the legitimacy of your leadership effectiveness. Because, if they don't trust you as a person—you're not really leading anybody!

Robert Shaw (1997) provides valuable insight into the act of trusting. Let's compare three statements to make sure that we understand what it means to *"trust"* someone:

1. **"I have confidence in Mr. Jones."** Confidence comes because of specific knowledge that is based on reason, fact, and frequently experience. Often, your confidence in someone has been validated over time.

AN INTROSPECTION

2. **"I have faith in Mr. Jones."** Your faith in someone may not be as strong as confidence because faith is given *in spite of* some circumstances, experience, evidence, or even just a feeling, that suggests you might want to use caution or even hold back. Absolute or "blind faith" can be a problem because it may be immune to contradictory information or facts. Just like in religion, faith can go beyond reason and be unshakable.
3. **"I trust Mr. Jones."** Trust is different from confidence and faith. Simply having trust in a person is a lot shakier than having experienced-based confidence in him/her, and trust's "faith component" is often much less than absolute. Trusting someone implies a much more fragile relationship. It simply means that you have some level of a combination of confidence, faith, and hope that that person (leader) will meet your positive expectations. You believe that that person (leader) will behave in a manner consistent, as far as possible, with your interests.

Of these three endorsements, trust is frequently the one most easily shattered.

When we do decide to extend trust, it has limits and thresholds (Shaw, 1997). This is because most of us prefer to extend our trust in small increments; we try to only give small chunks until it is clear who we are dealing with. Trust really becomes an issue for us when a person, maybe a leader or supervisor, has influence over something that is important to us—like our paycheck or our career.

Being trusted is a critically important leadership value. But it's not easy to achieve, because you can't mandate trust from people. You can't purchase it and you can't borrow it. Leaders must *earn* trust. And, very few people will ship their entire "trust allotment package" to you via overnight mail. It usually takes time and comes in small building blocks.

Why does trust usually come in small chunks? Because when we initially extend our trust we become vulnerable; trusting someone is about taking a risk. So, therefore, we try to manage our vulnerability by taking only small risks. We prefer small risks, because if we're wrong about the person, we could be disappointed or even harmed.

You may not realize it, but "trust evaluation events" occur all the time, both in our private and our professional lives. We are constantly examining, assessing, and then reassessing exactly who we can trust by asking ourselves:

- Is this person fulfilling my positive expectations?
- Is my trust well placed in this person?

After our assessments, we make important judgments about a person's (leader's) character. Is this individual inherently trustworthy? Should I trust him/her completely? Should I limit my trust, or extend none at all?

The crazy paradox is that trust can't grow *unless* we are willing to take a risk; a risk that may lead to our disappointment or harm.

So, as a leader, you must understand that trust firstly requires that you understand your subordinates' positive expectations of you. What do they *want* from you? What do they *need* from you? And how do you determine that?

AN INTROSPECTION

There is one time-tested but little-used method that I totally recommend. It may seem awkward (and sometimes is), but what worked for me was to ask the people I supervised: "Exactly what do you expect from me?" And then listen to their answers like your career is depending upon it. Obviously, this strategy works best early in your relationship or assignment.

Also, recognize that people's positive expectations of you can be explicit or implicit. An explicit expectation sounds something like, "Mary, I don't see any problem giving you off next Saturday for that wedding." Or, "Inspector, I'll have that report on your desk first thing Monday morning."

Mary and the inspector have now been put in the position of trusting you; they have a clear, explicit expectation of a positive outcome. Can I offer a caution to you? As a leader, don't shoot yourself in the foot by making *any* promises that you're not absolutely certain you can deliver on.

Your subordinates may also have implicit expectations of you, which tend to be much more complex and subtler. Who knows why they're like this? Maybe just because people are so complex in their inner thoughts and emotions. Or, maybe, simply because the previous leader did things a certain way and they assume that you will too. As a leader, try to be aware of any implicit expectations, both on you and the organization, and address them with truthfulness.

And, remember, people are all "trust-wired" differently. Some people are by nature more trusting than others. Others have had bitter experiences by extending too much trust too quickly; so, they don't do it anymore. A leader must recognize and respect those differences in people.

If someone doesn't seem to initially trust your leadership, it might have nothing to do with you. Somewhere along the line, this person may have been disappointed or even harmed by a leader whom he/she trusted. If you encounter someone like this, recognize this as a leadership *opportunity*. Your goal should be to respect the person for who he/she is and commit yourself to earning his/her trust. That person's past is just that: in the past. You should concentrate on forging a positive future together.

So, an extremely important question is: as a leader, how do you build and maintain a high level of trust? Through study, I noted that trust is founded on three basic imperatives (Shaw, 1997). Through careful observation and personal experience, I learned that to build and maintain trust, a leader must consistently:

- **Achieve results.** As the leader, you must get things done. You must be totally competent and perform *your* job at an elevated level. Those following you should never doubt your abilities.
- **Demonstrate concern for your team.** You must show by words *and by actions* that you truly care about your team—especially in the face of incentives or pressures to do otherwise.

AN INTROSPECTION

- **Act with integrity.** Day in and day out, in addition to always *doing the right thing*, you must keep all your promises and treat everyone with respect and fairness. In short, you must be a "good person."

If you damage, or worse yet, remove any one of these foundation legs, total trust in the leader can collapse and shatter—maybe forever.

Let me ask a frequent promotional exam type of question extracted from leadership textbooks: "What personal behavior of a leader is the biggest and quickest killer of trust?" Subordinates will always struggle to cope with this negative trait of a leader. Any guesses?

The answer is *inconsistency*!

From the subordinates' perspective, if trust is to be generated there must be predictability of behavior from the leader (Bennis and Nanus, 1985). Leadership requires consistency; effective leaders are steady people. The ability of the subordinates to accurately predict the leader's behavior with a high probability of success, assuming the leader is doing the "right" things, generates and maintains trust.

As a leader you cannot be up and down, right and left, or all over the place in your positions, behavior, and/or moods. No one will trust you.

DECIDING WHO LIVES—AND WHO DIES

It's not difficult at all for me to recall the anguish I felt standing on 11th Street commanding the operations at the Central Apartments Fire. I can relive just about every gut-wrenching

LEADERSHIP VALUES

moment of that hot, humid August night with so much smoke dampening the street—and so many lives on the line.

Our first alarm units responded to the fire at 12:37 AM and were met with a nightmare situation. The old structure was a fully occupied five-story apartment building, approximately 40' x 100', with a large open central staircase and twenty-eight apartment units. Most residents were asleep when a fire began in a concealed electrical pipe-chase in a third-floor hallway. With incredible speed, the fire extended horizontally and then upwards to the fourth and fifth floors producing extreme heat and thick, choking smoke. Eventually, the fire spread into the cockloft.

The first arriving units transmitted a second alarm within six minutes of their dispatch and the fire escalated all the way up to six full alarms. To provide some perspective, that's 25 engine companies alone. The response also brought numerous chief officers, ladder companies, medic units, heavy rescue, special operations companies, and miscellaneous apparatus.

The two most immediate challenges were to rescue all the trapped people, both inside the burning building and hanging out of the windows, and to launch an all-out, aggressive interior hoseline attack on the fire. So many people were only moments from death unless the firefighters could intervene. Seven people were rescued from portable ladders only seconds before their death while dozens of others inside the building

AN INTROSPECTION

were guided through the dense smoke and heat, or carried out of the building by firefighters.

I kept sending arriving company after company into the building as the rescue of trapped residents seemed like it would never end. By the fifth alarm, I began to commit some units to set up for an exterior attack; the building's total destruction seemed inevitable to me.

However, the thing I remember the most about that fire was being totally alone in shouldering the responsibility of deciding the exact moment to cease rescue operations. The fire had seized total control of the building with heavy flames now on floors two through five and bursting through the roof—and I still had approximately eighty-five firefighters inside the structure. To pull the firefighters out too soon would mean giving up on continued search and rescue operations and doom any still trapped, unconscious, or incapacitated residents to certain death. But to leave the firefighters inside the building much longer clearly raised the probability of *their* deaths in an eventual fiery collapse.

The decision was anguish. For, in reality, I was deciding who could live and who could die. No one at the command post offered any advice to me; even those who outranked me. They too knew what was playing out in front of our eyes.

I sensed a momentary lull in the portable radio traffic describing active rescue operations, and chose that moment to withdraw all the firefighters. I issued the formal order for an immediate, total emergency evacuation of the building. I contacted all the sector commanders and ordered their forces out. I instructed the Fire Communications Center to transmit the emergency evacuation signal over everyone's portable radio and the street-level fire engine air horns simultaneously blasted the emergency withdrawal signal. Although two firefighters were injured, none were killed that night.

Around 8 AM, I was relieved on the scene by the oncoming day-tour division commander. The fire was mostly out and remarkably, the building never collapsed. However, it was deemed "Imminently dangerous" and awaited a methodical demolition from the City's contractor crew under the direction of PFD fire investigators.

I drove home that morning sick with the thought of how many residents I had probably sentenced to death. How many charred bodies would the investigators find in the rubble? Would any of them be children? Would there just be three or four dead residents, or would it be revealed that I had abandoned ten or twenty people to perish in the fiery Hell? Amazingly, I crawled into my bed and fell asleep; I guess the extreme mental exhaustion of the seven-hour ordeal had taken its physical toll.

That night on the television news, it was reported that no bodies had been discovered—yet! The same result came at the end of the second day of our fire marshals carefully searching through the charred ruins. After several days, the contractor

AN INTROSPECTION

crew demolished the remainder of the burned-out structure. No bodies were discovered, and no reports of any missing residents came forth.

If you were to ask me why I picked that specific moment for the firefighters' withdrawal and not two minutes prior or two minutes later, I couldn't give you a detailed explanation. It had to be one of those gut feeling reactions that Teddy Roth so memorably seared into my soul many years prior (see the value of Decisiveness, Chapter #3)

Before reporting in for duty on my next scheduled shift, I stopped to attend an early mass with the nuns at old Saint Francis De Sales Church. On my knees, I thanked God for giving me that moment of strength to trust my own judgment on the evacuation call.

I was reminded once again of the very highest level of trustworthiness. That highest level goes beyond just correctly knowing when to trust other people; that greatest challenge and gift is *knowing when to trust your own judgment.*

LEADERSHIP VALUES

Seven are rescued in Center City fire
Dramatic rescues in Center City fire

Firefighters pulled seven people to safety in the blaze at 11th and Spruce.

By Natalie Pompilio, Robert Moran and Larry Fish
INQUIRER STAFF WRITERS

From the upper floors of the apartment building, people were hanging out their windows, screaming, with black smoke billowing from behind them. Flames were popping out of windows. One woman had tied a sheet around her radiator and appeared ready to try climbing down the five stories to safety.

On the street below, those who had made it out of the hallways while frantically calling for neighbors and pulling fire alarms to no avail watched in horror and screamed for help to come.

And it did.

Firefighter Joe O'Brien was one of the first to dash up a 35-foot ladder to the building's third floor. Through the smoke, he said, he could see a young man hanging from a window.

"He was panicking," said O'Brien, a firefighter for 12 years. O'Brien's ladder was a little short, but he pulled himself through the man's window. There, he said, he tried to calm the man down.

"I knew things were deteriorating rapidly and I had to get him and myself out of there,"

O'Brien said. "I knew it was a matter of minutes before the place was going to flash. But I didn't want him to know."

O'Brien wrapped his arms around the man and passed him to a second firefighter on the ladder. He followed.

Minutes later, the room "flashed" — filled with flames.

More than 150 firefighters from across the city responded to the six-alarm blaze at 11th and Spruce Streets about 12:30 a.m. yesterday. Rushing their ladders into the air, they pulled at least seven people to safety within minutes, then spent the next three hours battling a stubborn blaze.

"We had a lot of rescues. We definitely saved some lives," Deputy Fire Commissioner Lloyd Ayers said.

Firefighters chopped down doors to make sure residents were out and safe. They found a woman huddled in a hallway and pulled her from the building. In one apartment, Hanson said, a firefighter found a man walking around, disoriented. He pulled the man to the floor, and the pair crawled together through the apartment, down the hallway, and to the exit.

Battalion Chief Francis Hanson, a 33-year veteran, said the blaze "rates in the top five" he has dealt with.

"The amount of sheer work that had to be done while we were fighting the fire and the danger puts it up there," he said.

"At that point, the heat was so severe, if you stood up, you wouldn't be able to live," Hanson said.

No one was seriously injured in the blaze, but eight people, including two firefighters, sought treatment for smoke inhalation and other injuries at nearby Thomas Jefferson University Hospital, a hospital spokesman said. Two people were kept overnight.

But the building at 1034 Spruce — housing 28 apartments, almost all occupied, and the restaurants Islas, Jin House, and Where Else? on the bottom floor — was destroyed and must be torn down, officials said.

About 30 people were left homeless.

The top floor of the building next door was slightly damaged, and firefighters evacuated the north side of Spruce.

FROM *THE BULLETIN* AND *PHILADELPHIA DAILY NEWS*

AN INTROSPECTION

NOTE: Following this fire, the Department bestowed *five* Heroism Awards and *twenty-seven* Unit Citations to responding firefighters and paramedics for courageous actions under very dangerous conditions.

INTROSPECTION

- What grade would you give yourself on having people's trust?

- As a leader, do you have a clear and accurate understanding of your subordinates' expectations of you? How did you acquire that valuable knowledge?

- When you look at your team, is there one member who you quietly feel doesn't quite trust you completely? Why is that? Can you do anything about it?

- In work, what's your personal philosophy on making promises? Would everyone agree that "your word" is solid gold?

- Do you freely extend trust to others or are you more guarded in your actions? Would you like to change your behavior?

- Is your leadership consistent? Do your moods ever affect your leadership steadiness?

- **In examining the three foundation components for building subordinates' trust, is there *any* room for your personal improvement?**
  - Would everyone agree that you are totally competent?
  - Do you consistently show your subordinates by deeds, not just by words, that you truly care about their welfare?
  - Do you really demonstrate integrity daily?

CHAPTER 10

Pride

PRIDE IS THE LOFTY SELF-RESPECT AND SELF-ESTEEM THAT WE HOLD FOR OURSELVES. We generate pride ourselves; it comes from within us.

Justified pride in your group, office, company, division, unit, or organization can be a wonderful thing. It can serve as the second wind that carries you over the top, it can overcome weaknesses, and it can bond diverse interests. Pride can be the ultimate motivator.

There is nothing wrong with being proud. Pride is a great feeling; it brings us joy. You should have pride both in your personal accomplishments and, if you're a leader, in your group's achievements.

Pride is on display everywhere nowadays; and, there's no shortage of sources for it. We have company pride, school pride, ethnic pride, LGBTQ pride, and hundreds of other types.

LEADERSHIP VALUES

But, you must be careful because false pride can be dangerous and destructive. Even too much air pumped into a balloon will eventually burst it. An excessive amount of pride may be way out of balance with reality and this imbalance can distort some people's view of what's really going on. Haven't you met people in leadership positions who ignore the workplace reality? People who:

- Are unjustifiably confident in their skills and abilities.
- Greatly exaggerate their personal achievements and contributions.
- Grossly overestimate their value to their team or organization.

But, do you know what's even worse than publicly displaying these distortions? Some of these leaders may actually *believe* in their superiority.

Psychologists tell us that one visible manifestation of excessive, run-away pride is arrogance; which is a form of aggression. Arrogant people concentrate obsessively on themselves and achieving their goals. They are negatively focused to the point where they consistently disrespect, belittle, or even threaten the "lesser people" who they see as inhabiting their private world—and possibly taking attention away from them.

So, by all means: be proud of what you've achieved. But keep it under control. Make sure your pride is justified; keep the essential balance between your level of pride and reality.

From your formal education and life experiences, you probably recall some of the different theories on how to instill pride in people.

AN INTROSPECTION

But one thing that the experts all agree upon is that an individual must have an ample supply of self-respect and self-esteem. In other words, if you're the leader, you must *believe in yourself* before you can get your superiors, co-workers, or subordinates to believe in you.

And believing in yourself works best when you truly know yourself; which frequently begins with an honest self-assessment of your own strengths and weaknesses. Have you ever sat quietly and held an honest introspection in which you seriously reflected on your career—and your life? Just you, all alone, thinking the deepest of thoughts in a sincere effort to understand exactly who you are by:

- Knowing what your core values are.
- Knowing what you really believe in.
- Knowing what you are willing to fight for.
- Reflecting on any behavior that needs improvement.
- Deciding to improve.

It is essential for all leaders to maintain an appropriate level of pride; not too much, but not too little either. So, how does a leader stay grounded and well-balanced?

Above all, an effective leader must reside in the real-world; not in some type of Fantasyland where you're so good that you're positively convinced that you're without equal. You must make certain that the things you're proud of truly do merit your pride. I've found two methods that helped me to keep my level of pride justified and balanced.

First, practice being your own critic. Even after you have taken the bows and basked in the spotlight, make the time to honestly assess your own efforts and performance. Many times, even after a successful event, we'll be able to think of something that we could have done better for the next time. So, get in the habit of critiquing your own performance and obtaining some important take-away lessons for your future personal improvement.

My self-critiques last anywhere from sixty-seconds to, if any research is required, an hour. My most successful performance self-assessments come when I:

- Remember the purpose of the activity; it's supposed to be a helpful personal training exercise. The goal is to improve my performance—not kill my confidence or drive me to despair.
- Select the right time for the evaluation. Sometimes immediately after an event, my emotions can be too high to think clearly. In contrast, waiting too long usually diminishes the accuracy of my recollections.
- Analyze all areas of my performance, including, if warranted, my preparation efforts.
- Focus on both what I have done right and those areas where I need improvement. I take special note of repeated failures on the same issue.
- Seek the *specific* reasons for my failures. Is it a lack of knowledge? Am I communicating poorly? Is there a character tendency or flaw?
- Concentrate on personal behaviors that I *can* change and not waste time on issues that are beyond my control.
- Reflect on how my behavior affects others, positively or negatively.

AN INTROSPECTION

- Gain clear, *specific* "Lessons Learned" on how to improve my performance for the next time. After every extra alarm fire or emergency that I ever commanded as a chief officer, I logged my performance positives and negatives—and reviewed them periodically.
- Cut myself some slack by being content that I am, at least, moving in the right direction—even if still far from perfect.

Secondly, try to make everything in your professional life about *excellence*. It's easy to spot leaders who earnestly pursue excellence because they "autograph" every job, project, or assignment with it. Everything they touch; their tasks, reports, presentations, personal appearance, customer service. etc. produces a first-class result.

These special leaders believe that every assignment that they are given actually becomes a "self-portrait." And, if they complete the portrait in an excellent fashion, increased pride just follows along naturally. And the best part is that the pride is justified because these special leaders really are that good. Both the team and the bosses know it; and sometimes, even the "customers" know it. But, most importantly, the leaders know it.

ACE

After my promotion to captain, I floated from fire station to fire station for several months. Late one Friday afternoon, I received a call from the Deputy Chief informing me that I was being transferred to Engine Company 24 in South Philly.

LEADERSHIP VALUES

I was ecstatic that my first assignment as a commanding officer was going to be with a company that enjoyed a wonderful reputation throughout the PFD. At that time, Engine 24 was a hard-hitting, single engine, rock solid unit that had no ladder company housed with it to handle immediate ventilation, laddering, and rescue functions. This meant that the firefighters at 24's had to do it all; and they did it in a local area that repeatedly led the City in civilian fire deaths. As tragic as these mounting fire deaths were, they clearly pinpointed an area of the City for any firefighter who was seeking the highest level of "action."

I sensed the high honor of being named the captain of 24's, which only increased when the Chief informed me that the last four captains of Engine 24 had all been promoted to battalion chief directly out of that station.

When word spread of my transfer that weekend, I started receiving congratulatory calls from my friends and peers. But, many of the calls touched on a consistent point: "How lucky you are Gary, you'll be working the 'A' Platoon with Ace McCann," and "So, you're going to Ace McCann's platoon? How fortunate you are."

I had heard the firefighter's name around but never really paid attention to any specifics. So, I went to see my friend and previous boss, Lieutenant "Iron Mike" McBride, who I knew was a very proud alumnus of Engine 24. I told him of the numerous positive comments I was receiving on "this Ace McCann fellow."

AN INTROSPECTION

I asked Mike for some insight, "What's the story on this Ace guy? What can you tell me before I work with him for the first time?"

"He's just the best, Gar', the very best we have."

"The best *what*?" I asked.

The Iron Man took his time replying. I could see that he was seriously trying to formulate a helpful answer. Eventually, Mike said, "The best *everything*."

After my very first roll call formation at 24's, I made a few announcements and then dismissed the off-going platoon. I stood alone in front of my new team, Medic 14 and 24's "A" Platoon. I introduced myself while simultaneously scanning the crew. No one seemed to stand out as a larger-than-life, Paul Bunyanesque, heroic figure. Going down the straight formation line, I shook each firefighter's hand as he introduced himself.

Next-to-last in line, a 42-year old "regular-looking" man of medium build, medium height, with no obvious super-powers that I could detect extended his hand and said, "Welcome aboard, Cap. My name is Tom McCann, but most people call me Ace."

Later that morning, with everyone gathered in the small firehouse kitchen as sausage, eggs, and home fries grilled on the stove, I watched one of those common, loud, rollicking, back-and-forth, shouting over each other, "conversations" break out concerning the implementation of a new departmental policy. I just sat there silently, taking in the group dynamics. However, around the five-minute point in the verbal mayhem, Ace began to articulate an idea—and everyone instantly stopped speaking. I was stunned at the level of respect I had just witnessed.

As the weeks went by and turned into months, I got to know Ace very well. By that time, we had made some pretty tough jobs together, and that natural bonding that occurs between firefighters who have crawled hallways and taken a beating together developed. As a firefighter, he was simultaneously fearless, knowledgeable, inspirational, and fun to be with.

The courage and leadership that Ace exhibited during the worst of conditions were humbling to all of us. After our first wicked basement fire together, his aggressiveness made me wonder if he secretly possessed some type of a death wish. But, that notion went out the window during a kitchen critique immediately following the fire when Ace articulated the finer points of thermal balance and flashover indicators to our newer firefighters. *Damn, he probably knew more than me.*

Ace's personal quest for excellence didn't start and end on the emergency scenes. One day, I asked him to repaint the rear compartment of the fire engine. He went on to repaint that rear compartment *and* every compartment on the driver's side—by himself. Another day, I asked him to spend a half-hour reviewing pumper operations with Tommy and Bob, our two newer members. Ace spent an hour a day instructing them on

AN INTROSPECTION

the proper operation of the pumper—for a month. There *may* have been a few firefighters who were in Ace's elite class, but I had never seen anyone better.

On one occasion over beer and pizza while off-duty, I did get Ace to open up so I could glimpse what was driving that big heart of his.

"So, Ace, was there ever a time when you didn't drive yourself so hard to be the best?"

"I don't think so, Cap. As long as I can remember, I never took shortcuts or the easy way out. That's the way I was raised. My mother used to drum into me, 'Tommy, if it's worth doin'; it's worth doin' right.'"

I nodded in approval and replied, "Are you aware of the enormous positive impact your actions have on the platoon—in fact, the whole station?"

"Maybe. Yeah, I guess so. But, I don't act like this for anybody else. I'm hard-wired this way. I can't help it; I'm a very proud guy."

I responded, "I know that. Your pride and your character are beautiful things to be around. You raise all of us up."

"I appreciate that, Cap. But, like I said before, I act this way for me only. I feel like I have this constantly churning powerful engine inside me that just *compels* me to always raise higher, go further, and dig deeper than others. I want to be the best firefighter, the best father, the best person I can be. In work,

I want to be the first guy in, and the last guy out. When I go home after work, I need to feel—to *know*—that I gave everything I had."

"You know, Ace, in all these months we've worked together, I never heard you boast about any of the great things you've done; even your formal recognition events and achievements."

Ace paused and slowly returned his slice of pizza to the silver baking pan. For a second, he lowered his head in obvious deep thought. Then he responded, "Bragging? I could never do that. That would ruin everything. In my mind, it would tarnish or negate every good thing I ever did. I know it sounds crazy, but I guess I'm telling you that I have too much pride to boast."

I drank in the complexity of his last sentence and then smiled. I understood the genuineness and the depth of his pride.

"Hey, Cap, can we change the subject? I'm getting a little uncomfortable here. Let me order two more beers and we'll talk about you."

I came to realize that Ace was full of justified pride. He was extremely proud of his son, his Irish ancestry, his Catholic faith, the Philadelphia Fire Department, and especially being a member of 24's. He *loved* Engine 24.

Several years later, Ace was called upon to work in Headquarters as an Assistant Chief's aide for his long-time friend Joe McCarey. When Chief McCarey retired, Ace asked to return to active firefighting in the field forces. Headquarters

AN INTROSPECTION

graciously offered to assign him to whatever vacancy he chose. We were all surprised when Ace selected Engine 57's "C" Platoon in West Philly; we thought that he would want to slow down a bit in his remaining years. Engine 57 was nicknamed "The Battleship of the West" for very good reason; it was a high-pressure company getting a ton of nasty fires on a weekly basis. As the First Division, "C" Platoon Commander, I was delighted that Ace and I were going to be working together again.

Those first three months, I would see Ace frequently on the West Philly "All Hands" jobs and some extra alarms. I would make it a point to catch up on all his family news and we would reminisce and laugh about the great "old days" we spent together at Engine 24.

One tour of duty, 57's caught a brutal first-in structure fire around eight o'clock at night. Ace was the tip man and took a real shellacking. After the fire's knockdown, I looked at his fifty-something sagging demeanor and asked him if he was okay.

Ace just said, "Fine, Chief; no problem." His body indicated otherwise.

Several hours later, 57's again was first-in on a ripping fire in a four-story apartment building. When the fire was extinguished, I saw Ace with a soot-stained face and fiery red, watery eyes looking totally exhausted as he sat on the rear running board of 57's pumper with his bunker coat wide open.

LEADERSHIP VALUES

He told me that the heat on the upper floors was terrible and he just needed a few minutes to recover. I hoped he was right; but, for the first time since I'd known him, he did not look like the invincible warrior we had all come to know.

That morning, at 7 AM, an hour before we were to go off duty for four days, Ace called me in Division #1 Headquarters. He told me that on that apartment house fire he had "given up the tip." He was thankful that it was to another firefighter from 57's, but, none the less, it was the first time in his storied career he had ever given up the attack hoseline nozzle. He felt shame that he just couldn't will himself to advance further into the searing heat.

Dripping with raw emotion and seemingly near tears, Ace said, "It's over, Chief. I just wanted you to be the first to know. I'm going down to Headquarters tomorrow and sign my retirement papers. I ain't got it anymore. I don't belong here with these great guys."

I was totally shocked but reacted immediately, "Ace, so you had one bad night. It's happened to all of us somewhere along the line in our careers."

"Not to me, Chief. I gave up the tip for the first time in my life."

"Okay, I understand," I replied, "but, don't retire without giving this some more serious thought. I can get you out of 57's tomorrow. Let me call the Commissioner; we can move you to

AN INTROSPECTION

a slower company near your house. Or, how about the airport? You still have so much to offer—to all of us!"

"Nah, I appreciate it, Chief. But, it's over. I couldn't work in one of those slow companies. And the airport? Can you honestly see me at the airport? I'm not me anymore—or maybe I'm just a new me. And, I don't like this new me. These two jobs tonight have shown me that the old me is gone forever."

"Please hold off, Ace. We can talk in two or three days. We can go to lunch or meet anywhere you choose," I begged.

"I don't think you understand what I'm saying, Chief." His words dripped with emotion, "It's my pride. Maybe I *could* live without the respect of the other guys, but I *can't* live without respecting myself—who I am—who I've been all these years. I feel embarrassed to tell you that it's all about my pride, but it's the truth. This same pride that has sustained me and pushed me for over thirty years is now telling me, loud and clear, that's it's over. As a friend, I'd like you to understand and be the first to wish me well."

I felt numb. After several seconds of silence had passed, with my voice cracking and my eyes beginning to well up, I simply said, "God speed, Ace. God speed, my friend."

Firefighter Thomas "Ace" McCann did retire the next afternoon. On that day, not only did the Department lose an incredible, living asset—I lost a personal hero.

LEADERSHIP VALUES

But, from that experience, I learned the enormous power of pride in shaping who we truly are. For many people walking among us, pride is the overwhelming, number one driving force in guiding their actions; good *or* bad. Ace had given me his final lesson in leadership—and life; *never* underestimate what actions a person will take to accommodate his/her personal level of pride.

MY FIRST COMMAND—ENGINE COMPANY #24 AND MEDIC UNIT #14
20TH AND FEDERAL STREETS, SOUTH PHILADELPHIA, 1975

AN INTROSPECTION

INTROSPECTION

- Where are you on the personal pride scale? Too much? Too little?

- Is your level of pride correctly balanced with reality?

- In what ways do you demonstrate your pride?

- What three achievements in your life are you most proud of? Do you publicly demonstrate that pride in any way or choose to keep it within?

- Have you delivered any self-portraits that didn't make you proud? Why did you allow it to happen?

- Are you regularly and honestly self-critiquing your own performances? If you are a leader and you are awarding yourself all straight A-pluses, you are probably performing the critique process incorrectly.

- Are you aware of all your personal behavior areas that could use improvement? Are you actively moving toward improvement?

CHAPTER 11

Compassion

COMPASSION IS THE SORROW OR PITY THAT WE FEEL FOR THE MISFORTUNES OF OTHERS; the key word is *"feel."* I hope that all of you have a large capacity to feel, to be human. Because I assure you that there are unlimited opportunities for leaders to demonstrate compassion in today's world.

Sooner or later, most of us get to see misfortune and grief up close. Sometimes, the view is even more frequent and more intense if you're in a leadership position. Like it or not, ready or not, leaders are frequently present in other people's darkest hours; in an instant, leaders can often become "our brother's keeper." Uncontrolled circumstances where one person is in desperate need of kindness or a helping hand have a way of meshing the lives of people and leaders together.

Leaders of all types should be mindful that some of the people they will come in contact with tomorrow or next month will truly

AN INTROSPECTION

be experiencing the very worst moment, or the very worst period, of their lives. They can be experiencing real pain... real anguish... real sadness. For the leader, it may be just a rainy Thursday, two hours until quitting time. But for these unfortunate souls, their world may be truly crumbling. It is exactly in these specific moments that leaders must recognize the priceless *opportunity* that they have to perform a meaningful human act of unforgettable compassion that will more deeply display their true leadership values and character.

Have you given any thought as to how you are going to develop and enhance your personal levels of compassion, empathy, tolerance, and understanding of people in your role as a leader? It's important because many subordinates take their cue from the leader's behavior. I'll give you a hint: insincere lip service won't get the job done. Sometimes, words alone fall short; frequently, compassion for others is about doing something.

Speaking of doing something, I would suggest that as a leader, you not be too slow in wiping a person's slate clean. Heaven knows, some of us have benefited from someone who really cared, someone who took a risk on us, someone who gave us a second chance. Don't lose sight of how many times *you* have benefited from forgiveness or a slate wiped clean. It must work both ways; being the leader does not entitle you to have selective memory function.

If somebody is in your personal "dog house," make sure that *you* put him/her there and you really believe that he/she has *earned* that distinction. Don't fill up your dog house by automatically buying into

LEADERSHIP VALUES

other people's water-cooler, rumor mill stories. When you are making a character assessment of someone, find out for yourself. It's too important a decision to leave for others. The larger your capacity for true leadership is, the smaller the dog house you will need.

A major component of compassion is forgiveness. I have found through experience that one of the heaviest things in life to carry around every day is a grudge. And it's even heavier if you are in a position of leadership.

I have to qualify my statements, so I don't misrepresent my level of kindness. I never, for example, had a loved one mugged in a robbery who ended up in a hospital ICU—or even worse. I confess that I'm not exactly sure how forgiving I would be to that. However, I have suffered my share of major kicks in the groin in my personal and professional life. On numerous occasions, I have fallen victim to the lowest of unfair and/or below-the-belt blows. So, on that specific level, I can speak firsthand about forgiveness. And I've found that carrying a grudge is a time-consuming, energy-draining, focus-robbing, negative activity that can pull on a leader's character like a sack full of rocks. Most leaders should, and *do*, have more important things to worry about than old or emerging grudges.

Initially, I misunderstood forgiveness; I thought it mandated a total reconciliation and rebuilding toward the previous relationship status. And in many situations, I wasn't up to that. But, that doesn't need to be the case; achieving those plateaus are often impossible. To forgive simply means to stop feeling anger and resentment.

AN INTROSPECTION

So, forgiveness becomes not just about the one who harmed me, but forgiveness can also be about me. And selfishly—for me. I have learned that when I forgive someone, I am actually giving *myself* a gift of freedom from pain and anger and carrying around the grudge.

Because when you've got a real grudge, you have to take it everywhere. You must take it to the office, to the factory, to the mall, to the ball game—even to church. You can't leave your grudge at home because you never know when you'll have to open your "quick-release grudge bag" and activate your negative stuff. What if you unexpectedly run into an "enemy" while grocery shopping? You don't want to be caught off-guard... and then what? Have to be civil...or polite... or decent?

Embarrassingly, I've learned from personal experience that maintaining your grudges is not a freebie. If you're going to actively "work your grudge" as a leader, it will cost you. You'll pay the heavy price of giving up your time, your energy, and tons of your emotion.

When you are actively working your grudge, it remains prominent in your frontal lobe; it's always there. I've learned that when someone hurts me, I have *already* given him/her power to touch me in some emotional way. And me hanging on to my pain and frequently thinking about him/her, or the incident, every day, just gives him/her even more power over me. It's like I'm giving him/her free rental space in my head!

Here's my point: leaders cannot function at their best if someone is holding emotional power over them. I know it can be extremely difficult to forgive someone or give someone a second chance. Believe me, I know because I "medaled" in grudge-holding. If you can find a way to let it go, you will discover that you're greatly expanding your capacity for genuine leadership.

Let me give you another related tip: as a leader, be acutely aware of exactly how you treat the people *who treat you the worst*. Everybody is usually watching your reaction(s) to situations like these, and making judgements. They are drawing conclusions about *your* character. So, when you seek revenge on Joe or publicly scream and lose control with Tom, you're clarifying your character for everyone. Your actions may have an unintentional result, but one holding real significance; especially for those who work for you. What would make them think that they would be treated any different if they angered you?

Keep in mind that if you throw a temper tantrum and start screaming, you are acknowledging to everyone that the situation is just too intense for your ordinary coping skills. You don't have any other "tools" in your "leadership bag"; yelling is all you've got. In *self*-control lies the secret to controlling other people. To command others—you must first learn to command yourself.

This quote from Aristotle is my favorite about anger: "Anybody can get angry, that is easy. The difficulty lies in getting angry... with the *right* person... to the *right* degree... for the *right* purpose... at the *right* time... and, in the *right* way. That is not within everyone's power—and it is not easy."

The quote prompts us to ask an important question. What about those leaders who:

AN INTROSPECTION

- Misplace and misdirect their anger toward the wrong person because it's more convenient... or (cowardly) safer?
- Exhibit a level of anger that has no sense of proportion?
- Are less than honest about the *real* cause of their anger?
- Display ill-timed outbursts that are either much too quick or much too late?
- Show child-like anger rather than acting like a fully developed adult?

Aristotle's advice is priceless—especially for a leader.

UNDERNEATH DAY

I remember with regret how I struggled to live up to meeting some of the values of true leadership character during my first year as an officer. Transferred to Engine 68, I had received a wonderful assignment in West Philly. I landed with a terrific platoon of firefighters and worked for one of the finest captains to ever wear the PFD blue serge uniform; George Lieb.

From the first day of my assignment to 68's, Captain Lieb welcomed me, guided me, mentored me, inspired me, and looked out for me. Although he was twenty years my senior, we connected on every level. He was an encyclopedia of knowledge, a masterful story teller (always offered with a valuable lesson to learn), and a granite block of integrity. Everyone in the department respected his character, ability, and judgment; in fact, I

LEADERSHIP VALUES

noticed that on several occasions even the Fire Commissioner would call him to discuss an issue.

I probably fooled everyone into thinking that I was an ideal officer during my first year as a lieutenant at 68's; competent and composed of good character. I was very popular with my subordinates and was always invited to the firefighters' parties, barbecues, and other affairs. I played on the battalion softball and touch-football teams with the guys and enjoyed going out for an after-shift drink. I valued my popularity very much.

That was the problem. Too many times, my decisions would rest solely on what perceived effect they would have on my popularity. I was terribly weak. But, far worse than my character weakness was my propensity to lie whenever required to protect my popularity.

I never issued an unpopular order during that first year without shifting the blame to someone else. The lies allowed me to continue being "one of the guys." It would be so comforting if I could tell you that I didn't really understand the implications of my behavior; but it would not be true. I knew; I just couldn't picture myself existing as one of those many officers I encountered who no one liked. To severely complicate matters, I engaged in this distasteful behavior despite the fact that I truly desired to excel in every aspect of my new leadership role.

One morning at roll call, after consulting the station housework schedule, I informed my platoon that they would

AN INTROSPECTION

be required to clean the underneath of the fire engine. "Underneath Day" was a controversial task left over from a bygone era in the Department. It called for firefighters to crawl under the fire engine with kerosene-soaked rags and remove the accumulated dirt from the chassis. Allegedly, it was also supposed to be done to spot loose bolts, leaks, and other mechanical problems. The unpleasant task was used frequently by some officers as an effective disciplinary tool. It was an ugly, dirty, nasty job that, although still listed on the schedule for quarterly maintenance, most officers ignored.

When my platoon members asked me why the task was to be done, I replied, "I know; it's crazy. But, that's what Captain Lieb instructed me to get done today." The captain had never made any such statement to me. Once they heard that Captain Lieb ordered it done, they went to work and did their usual excellent job.

Lying in bed at home that night, I was overcome with so many emotions as I finally acknowledged the motivation and consequences of my horrible behavior. Suddenly, I was panicked that someone would bring up Underneath Day to Captain Lieb and this particular lie would explode in my face and reveal my true identity. I vowed that it would end here.

Even though I was not due into work until 6 PM, I drove to 68's the next morning at 9 AM to confess to Captain Lieb what I had done and what I had become. My fear of how he would

LEADERSHIP VALUES

react was secondary to my compelling need to come clean and hopefully start "leading" anew.

Captain Lieb was surprised to see me standing in the office doorway over eight hours before my shift started.

"Hi, what are you doing here so early? C'mon in. What's up?" he asked.

I guess he noted my body language and downward fixed eyes and immediately knew something was troubling me.

"Sit down. What's wrong? Are you okay?"

It was a very dark half hour for me as I sat in front of him and detailed my year-long pattern of deceitful behavior concluding with blaming yesterday's Underneath Day on him. I can recall trembling slightly as the words left my mouth; I guess shame can do that to you. At the conclusion, I told Captain Lieb that I would understand—and deserve—any negative reaction he had towards me and that no matter what he said or did, the weakness and the lying were all over for me.

He took a few seconds to reflect on everything that I had said. His first words shocked me.

"Welcome aboard, Gar'. Welcome to the real officers' corps. I must tell you that I had no inkling whatsoever that you were struggling so much internally. I don't think anybody else here does either. But I'm telling you that this is an important day for you. *Today* is the day that you really become a leader."

AN INTROSPECTION

He continued from behind the desk while I was now able to look directly at him, "This whole leadership development process of going from being a firefighter one day and becoming a genuine leader the next day always takes time. It's a journey for each of us. We all have different paths to travel; and we all have different timetables. Don't you think that I struggled in the beginning? Some officers learn to stand on their own two feet relatively quickly while sadly others never reach that point. We have some officers who spend their entire career of twenty or thirty years acting as you just described—or worse! It's so sad."

And then, Captain Lieb rolled his chair to the side of the desk to be even closer to me and said, "So this is what I want you to do. I want you to always remember this day and this conversation—because it's a gift. It's a priceless gift of maturity that you've given to yourself. Today, Gary,... today you have become an officer in the Philadelphia Fire Department. You are now willing to accept *everything* that comes with being a true leader."

Driving back home I was consumed with the realization of how lucky I was. Lucky that my cowardly behavior had apparently gone unnoticed; lucky that Captain Lieb was in my life; and extremely lucky that I was going to get another chance at true leadership.

LEADERSHIP VALUES

That evening, at the 6 PM roll call, I was startled when, in front of both the "B" and "C" Platoons, Captain Lieb said, "I want to thank the "C" Platoon for the great job you guys did yesterday cleaning the underneath of the pumper. I know it's been a while, but for safety's sake, I just wanted someone to get under there and take a good look."

Then he shook my hand and said, "Thanks."

In that moment, I was placed on the receiving end of a compassionate act that would stay with me all the days of my life. I had been given a front row seat in experiencing what it actually feels like when someone understands you, empathizes with you, and demonstrates genuine tolerance and compassion towards you. I spent the rest of my career trying to honor Captain Lieb by emulating his compassion for others.

And, equally important, wherever the Department assigned me after that day, I always took my lumps—standing on my own two feet. I knew that any criticism, loneliness, or heartache that resulted from me fulfilling my duty was far more bearable than knowing I was a fraud.

AN INTROSPECTION

MY 1974 "EXTENDED FAMILY" – ENGINE #68, PLATOON "C"

(LEFT TO RIGHT). TOP ROW: BERNIE MCGUIRE, AL PONZIO, AUGIE OLIVIERI, BUD MCLAUGHLIN. BOTTOM ROW: ED JOWELL, BOB BOYLAN, LT. APPLEBY, CURTIS DENT, GEORGE KIMMEL

LEADERSHIP VALUES

INTROSPECTION

- How would you rate your level of compassion?

- Is your personal dog house so full it looks like the County SPCA?

- Are you currently carrying around one of those less than life altering event grudges (maybe a work event?) in which someone is currently renting free space in your head? Do you know what I wonder; are you on his/her mind to the same extent? What if he/she *never* even thinks of you?

- Do you have that rare leadership ability to put yourself in another's shoes? Doesn't empathy make understanding that person's behavior a little easier? And, doesn't that understanding help to make you a more effective leader?

- Are you a "yeller" when things don't go your way? Does yelling *ever* help the situation?

- Do you ever take your anger or frustration out on people who do not deserve it? Why?

- Where do you stand on extending second chances to people: always, never, or it depends on the situation?

CHAPTER 12

Loyalty

LOYALTY IS FAITHFULNESS to that which you are bound to by pledge, duty, responsibility, or, just as strongly, friendship or love. When you are loyal, it means that you maintain a steadfast relationship to some*thing* or to some*one* in the face of temptation to take the easy way out.

If there were no temptations, fears, or character flaws, we would all be loyal subjects all the time. We would never let down our family, friends, co-workers, bosses, subordinates, or the organization.

Today's leaders sometimes end up having to address multiple loyalties. If you are a leader, everybody wants or needs your loyalty: your team or unit, your organization, your "customers," your superiors, and your "extended family"—which is your subordinates.

But perhaps, the most difficult loyalty of all to maintain is loyalty to *yourself* and to your personal values. Remaining true and faithful to what you personally believe in all the time is far from easy. In fact, it's close to impossible for some people. Here's why; to be a genuinely loyal person, you should:

- Be a good listener.
- Use your integrity as the best proof of your loyalty.
- Stand up for others, especially when they're not present.
- Refrain from talking behind the back of someone who is close to you.
- Dissent in private (if possible) and support the team in public (if possible).
- Avoid hanging your team's dirty laundry out for others to see, except if morally impossible.
- Accept that what you *least* want to hear or say is often what you *most* need to hear or say.
- Refuse to let anyone take advantage of your loyalty; it's supposed to be a balanced two-way street of mutual fairness and respect.
- Understand the difference between servitude in which you're under the total control of someone else and have no freedom versus loyalty, which offers you a choice.
- Perhaps most importantly, remember that you cannot receive loyalty if you never give it.

Although I haven't figured out a precise mathematical equation yet, loyalty seems to me to be something that's adversely affected by both time and distance. Some (weak) people find it much easier to be

AN INTROSPECTION

loyal to someone "in the moment" or close by. When your loyalty stays unwavering despite the barriers of time and distance, it's genuine.

Loyalty can be confusing, especially as a leader. That's because multiple loyalties can cause conflict and confusion within all of us. Conflict, because it's possible that what's best for the customers may not be best, at that time, for the organization. What's best for your subordinates may not be best for your boss. What's best for you personally may be best for no one else.

Many new leaders experience loyalty conflicts in the beginning; other leaders are tormented with loyalty conflicts throughout their careers. Sadly, I have found there are no easy ways to resolve these conflicts. The best thing to do if you start to feel loyalty confusion is to stay loyal to your internal compass by focusing and acting on your core values. Frequently, that focus in examining what you personally stand for will both clarify and prioritize your loyalty obligation(s).

And consider this bit of sobering reality; someday, as a leader, you may desperately need loyalty from your subordinates. A situation may arise in which you need their full trust and compliance and, for whatever reason, you won't be able to fully explain the need for that trust and compliance at that particular moment. Uh-oh!

That is why it's wise to cultivate loyalty from your team members and allies *now*—during any so-called down time. Because sometimes when loyal support is required the most, it is far too late for the leader to start creating it.

How does a leader cultivate loyalty from team members during down time? The cultivation must begin with you never taking their loyalty for granted and then working to give them genuine reasons to respect and hopefully like you. Specific loyalty-building activities from a leader could include:

- Acknowledging good work performance, both publicly and privately.
- Attempting to know each team member on a deeper level.
- Discussing and connecting on common values and goals.
- Seeking opportunities to collaborate directly.
- Connecting team members to other solid people in your sphere.
- Discovering their less obvious work problems and issues and attempting to resolve them.
- Extending, where possible, consideration (favors!) for a personal need. Yes, I do mean the occasional bending of a rule.

All these activities may help a leader by building trust and loyalty *before* the inevitable crisis occurs.

Speaking of crises, there are lots of definitions out there attempting to define what a crisis is. As a leader, you're bound to ask yourself, "How will I know for sure when we're at the *true* crisis point?" Something that I have found first-hand to be accurate: during a true crisis, *nobody* is stepping forward to offer you any advice on how to do your job. They're all just standing back and looking to you. I'm betting that some of you have been there too; you've lived this definition.

Earlier I referenced the subordinates as a leader's extended family. I really believe in this concept. And, it's especially true in high

AN INTROSPECTION

performance organizations such as the military and public safety. A "family" is any group comprised of kindred spirits or close relationships; blood relationship may have no bearing on what defines a family. In some organizations, that "family feeling" is a cherished value; top leadership goes to great lengths to preserve and build a "family spirit."

Do you think of your organization as a family? After all, with a promotion to a leadership position, doesn't a person become the head of a little family, (a section, unit, office, branch, squad, platoon or division) within a bigger family? And we certainly know what the heads, the leaders, of families do for all their family members. The family leaders are supposed to watch over their family members; they protect them and guide them. In short, effective leaders *care* about all their family members.

OK, so you get a promotion and are suddenly deemed a leader and installed as a head of a family. And now the organization asks you to immediately start caring about four or six, or several dozen people, who you may never have seen before in your life.

Worse yet: you realize that *you're* going to be held accountable for *their* performance. This might make you uncomfortable; you may have one person on your team whom you've pegged immediately as a loser or a problem child. Maybe you got that feeling from a first impression, some water cooler gossip, or from a "heads-up" phone call from an acquaintance. But you've done no real personal investigation. So, does this person—or this relationship—deserve less respect, less attention, or less commitment from you?

LEADERSHIP VALUES

Many so-called losers and problem children got that way because nobody ever really cared about them. Maybe they never had a leader as good as you before; so, *give them a chance.* While it's often easier as a leader not to care, not to be inclusive, and not to display your loyalty—it's not right.

So, keep yourself above all the destructive games that go on in so many organizations today. Take that age-old advice our mothers gave us: *"Treat people like you want to be treated."* There are dozens of leadership books that devote entire chapters to the wisdom of this one sentence, but Mom's simple words nailed it. She knew how important mutual respect is in this world.

How would you like to work for a leader who not only espouses family values, but who seeks to build, to the degree possible, a family environment in the work place? Imagine that: a genuine extended family feeling in the Financial Aid Office, at the 19th Police District, in the shipping department—wherever! Where the leader's concern for his/her "family" manifests itself through a spirit of camaraderie.

Now, depending on where you currently work, you may not experience much camaraderie. Camaraderie is a union; a bonding based on shared experiences, fellowship, goodwill, friendship, mutual respect, and loyalty. As a leader, have you given any thought as to what your role will be in developing or fostering camaraderie in your team?

Additionally, to what degree are you responsible for your team's morale: totally, significantly, minimally, or not at all? Better yet, let me rephrase the question, "How does your current immediate supervisor affect your morale?" Do you ever tell anyone about your boss? So, the point to be made is: do you really expect it to be different for your subordinates? How can they eliminate you from their world?

Accept it: as a leader, you are a big factor in people's lives. A promotion guarantees you what textbooks refer to as an "increased sphere of influence." Because, as we've discussed before, with that new title and pay raise comes power and responsibility—and you must choose how you want to use that power and responsibility.

What do you want to bring to your team? You can bring camaraderie, comfort, joy, and good feelings to at least an entire unit or office. Or, you can bring anger, stress, disappointment and tons of bad feelings and dysfunction. As a leader, you must never forget, minimize, or ignore your effect on people's lives.

A BRICK TO THE FOREHEAD AND OTHER LEADERSHIP ADVICE

One of my most challenging acts while serving as the Department's Director of Training at the Fire Academy was to replace my enormously talented and dedicated deputy director who was transferring back to the field forces. Bill Shouldis had been with me from my first day at the Academy, and was a driving force behind so many of the positive things that were happening. I didn't know how I'd ever get someone of his high caliber to serve as my number one wingman.

LEADERSHIP VALUES

Among the battalion chiefs who requested consideration for the coveted staff position was Bruce Cowden. I had never worked directly with Bruce, but I had a terrific relationship with his older brother Bob. Bob was also a battalion chief and worked for me in North Philly's Third Battalion. No one would guess that they were third-generation PFD brothers. Bob was outgoing, charismatic, and beloved by his assigned troops. Bruce's strengths were in other areas. But, everyone agreed that they were both extraordinarily competent fireground commanders and men of the very highest integrity.

My interview with Bruce was unlike the sessions held with the other applicants. Quite noticeably, he spent a lot of time listening to my thoughts, my preferences, my needs, and my vision. He didn't interrupt me, nor did he attempt to "sell" me with his impressive credentials. The only promise he made was to work hard. It was almost like he was interviewing *me* to see if he liked the situation.

Some of my friends advised me that Bruce was "all business and could get pretty intense." They also stressed that "having fun" was not a priority for him. But fun aside, Bruce seemed like a perfect match for where I wanted to take the Department's training and education efforts. I gave him the job and we spent six wonderful years working side-by-side.

It wasn't long after we began working together that I experienced Bruce's particular demonstration of loyalty. Whenever

AN INTROSPECTION

he felt that I had screwed up, he would privately and respectfully call me out on it. Every time.

After a month together, his first criticism of me came at the end of a busy day with the two of us sitting in my office.

"Chief," he said, "I think your leadership style could use some improvement."

"What do you mean?" I asked.

"I think your preference for delivering orders gently wrapped up in a gift box with a bow on it doesn't work all the time. You see, Gene (the Academy Operations Officer) and I get you. We know that when you begin a phrase with 'Wouldn't it be nice if....' or 'Is there any way we could....', you're not really asking a question or bouncing things off us. We know that you're gently telling us what you want done; you're giving us firm direction—orders."

Reluctantly, I said, "Tell me more."

Bruce continued, "This frustration you feel when guys don't pick up on your hints or suggestions is caused by your own doing. Most of us get your style and it creates a nice working atmosphere here. But, some of these guys on our staff need a brick to the forehead. They really *believe* that you're just thinking out loud or offering a suggestion. You never led by suggestions or hints on the fireground; you made everything you wanted accomplished crystal clear. I think some of that emergency scene style of leadership has a place here."

LEADERSHIP VALUES

"Do you mean change my style completely?" I replied.

"No. I'm just saying that you'd be better off to stop blaming them and do a better job yourself in identifying who requires a brick to the forehead versus those of us who correctly pick up on your hints. You'd actually be doing yourself a favor by reducing your frustration."

Point taken by me.

During my time as an officer and most especially when I became a chief officer, I formed the habit of asking people to let me know if I could help them with anything. Most of the time, I meant the offer; but sometimes I uttered the words because I felt it provided me with a good image, boosted team morale—and, embarrassingly, it made me feel good about myself. I was lucky that people did not frequently take me up on it. And, on those occasions when I was asked for specific help, it usually came from someone who I was happy or obligated to assist.

One afternoon, Bruce and I attended a meeting at Headquarters along with many non-uniformed staff administrators. Following the meeting, we were talking with a senior civilian staff member named Joe with whom I had a pleasant professional relationship. Joe and I would interact once or twice a month on Fire Academy business.

Joe disclosed that he was entering the hospital in a few days for major surgery and detailed his upcoming operation and his required convalescence.

AN INTROSPECTION

Before we parted to drive back to the Academy, I said, "Joe, we wish you the best of luck. Let me know if I can do anything for you."

He said, "Thanks," and off Bruce and I went.

The next afternoon around 4 PM, Bruce entered my office to find me sitting behind my desk looking rather glum.

"What's wrong, Chief? Are you okay?"

"Do you remember yesterday when I asked Joe to let me know if he needed anything?"

"Sure," Bruce said, "you say that to almost everybody."

"Well, he just called. Guess what he wants," I said.

Slowly shaking his head from side-to-side as he seriously pondered the question, Bruce said, "I have no idea what he could want from you."

I gritted my teeth and through the tightest of jaws, I said, "He wants my blood!"

"What! Your blood? What do you mean?"

"He wants me to drive to the main branch of the Red Cross tomorrow and donate a pint of blood which will be credited to his medical insurance account."

"Are you serious? What did you say?"

I said, "Okay."

"Wow. Do you want to give your blood for this guy? I didn't even know you two were friends."

"No, we're not friends. I talk to the guy once or twice a month and it's always about Academy stuff. I've never seen him socially in my life. I don't really know anything about him."

Bruce exploded with such loud laughter that he had to sit down. He kept on belly-laughing so hard that I even cracked a wide smile. I nodded my understanding of what had occurred.

"You know, Chief, I've often wondered if you were always totally sincere in your offers to help people out. I mean, it's a beautiful thing you do but I've seen you offer your help to some pretty questionable characters; even an asshole or two."

"Really?"

"Oh yeah. Well, can you blame him for taking you up on your offer? After all, you did say it."

I replied with a tinge of anger, "I know I said it, but I just feel like he took advantage of me. I'll do it. I gotta do it, but I really don't want to give my blood for this guy. Don't you feel that his request crossed over the line?"

Bruce answered, "Chief, if you really want to know whose fault this situation is—go in the bathroom and look in the mirror."

Point taken by me, painfully.

Several weeks later, I was forced to deal with an out-of-state vender who was touting a new type of "miracle firefighting foam" that would extinguish building fires ten times faster than the "regular" water we used from our city mains and

AN INTROSPECTION

pumpers. Of course, it was a sham. The product was not only worthless, but extremely expensive. Worse, the company's CEO was a shameless, soulless charlatan whose penchant for greed was his only notable attribute.

Under the Commissioner's direction, I had the product tested extensively, both at the Fire Academy and out in the field with two of our busiest engine companies. All the claims of the foam company were proven fraudulent. And, as the Department's point of contact, I had several very unpleasant conversations with the arrogant, delusional CEO.

But the PFD had a problem: the start-up company had the strong backing of several powerful Washington, D.C. politicians. To his credit, the Fire Commissioner stood up to a United States senator and other political hacks in refusing to commit the City to purchase the product. The mayor, under significant pressure himself, asked the fire commissioner to run "one last test" at the Fire Academy in front of a new group of observers.

We all met in the Fire Academy's drill yard one morning and formed an informal circle by the burn-pits while the mayor's aide organized introductions. Bruce and I were the only two Fire Department representatives. When the foam company CEO extended his hand for me to shake, I just silently glared at him. It was an awkward moment for the group for sure. The mayor's aide noted the slight, quickly took control, and moved on to complete the introductions.

LEADERSHIP VALUES

We ran several live burn tests that morning comparing the miracle foam to plain old Philadelphia tap water. The results weren't even close; the miracle foam was crap and everyone saw it.

As Bruce and I walked back to the main campus building, he asked me why I didn't shake the CEO's hand.

"Because he's a piece of shit. You know that; I've told you about every one of our face-to-face or telephone encounters. He's a greedy, egotistical scumbag just out to make a buck."

Bruce didn't say a word, but I sensed he had something more he wanted to say.

"What's on your mind? Did you have a problem with me not shaking his hand?" I asked.

"To be honest, I was surprised at your action. I understand completely your well-deserved disdain for this asshole, but I think you let your personal feelings override the situation. All those people seeing you in uniform for the first time felt, understandably, that you represent the Philadelphia Fire Department. So, when you refused to shake the guy's hand, it meant that the Philadelphia Fire Department was refusing to offer even the slightest bit of common courtesy. I just think it made us look petty."

I stopped walking and we turned to face each other.

Before I could speak, Bruce said, "Hey, it's no big deal to me, Chief. I'm totally on your side. I was just surprised because

AN INTROSPECTION

I thought you were a bigger person than that. I thought you knew when you put that uniform on that you frequently speak and act for *all* of us. Like it or not, you represent all of us. And people are drawing conclusions about all of us based upon your behavior."

Point taken by me, very painfully.

Bruce's special application of loyalty also revealed itself to me one day when one of my senior staff officers at the Academy asked if I could give him a ride home. I was happy to oblige; Mike was one of the finest officers ever assigned to the Training Division. He was talented, authentic, and incredibly dedicated. And, just as important to me, because of our shared West Philly firefighting history, he always gave it to me straight.

Driving home, we chatted about our families for a while. Then I asked Mike, "How are you guys making out with Bruce?"

"He's tough, Chief. I get along fine with him, but he takes his job very seriously. It's pretty much all business—all the time."

"Is that a problem for the staff?" I asked.

"Not really; it's clear that he just wants us to be the best we can. Because of that, he's calls us out on every little screw-up we make. And, he keeps throwing these new tasks and goals at us. There's no let up."

"Like what?"

"Well, Monday he told us that we're all going to have to revise our testing content for the four main cadet curriculum sections. He said it's because we're going to a revised system of testing the cadets every Friday at two-week intervals. We've had the same cadet testing system in place from even before I got here. I understand that the system is a little disjointed, but I think on the whole it still works. This revised two-week approach is going to cause a lot of work for all of us."

"Mike, that order came from me. I'm the one who wants the changes. The current system is much too fragmented for me; I want it to be more structured and symmetrical."

Mike was surprised, "Oh, he didn't say the order came from you. He just said, 'This is what has to be done,' and gave us some guidelines and time frames."

We both took a moment to digest what was said. Then, Mike told me of another upsetting order that Bruce had delivered to the staff three weeks prior. I was stunned.

"Mike, that order came from me too. Didn't Bruce tell you guys that I wanted to make that change? It's all my idea."

"No, Chief. We all thought it was from him."

For the next few moments, as the car continued toward home, Mike and I didn't speak. No doubt, we both were beginning to understand and appreciate the essence of Chief Cowden's value system—and loyalty.

In the full six years that we worked together, Bruce continued to provide me with "character tune-ups" whenever he felt I did something wrong or was about to make an error. Very

AN INTROSPECTION

few people enjoy being criticized, especially by a uniformed subordinate. It was never pleasant for me; some of his feedback caused me pain, embarrassment, and/or deep reflection.

But I knew that Bruce liked me, respected me, and believed in me. Therefore, I understood that his criticisms were always delivered for my best interests. Bruce demonstrated his remarkable loyalty to me by *always* telling me the truth, whether I asked for it—or not!

He reinforced my understanding that sometimes both giving *and* receiving genuine loyalty can be painful in the moment; but it always benefits us in the long run.

PHILADELPHIA FIRE ACADEMY LEADERSHIP TEAM 1993–1999. (LEFT) BATTALION CHIEF BRUCE COWDEN; (CENTER) AUTHOR; (RIGHT) CAPTAIN GENE JANDA

PHOTO COURTESY OF THE PHILADELPHIA FIRE DEPARTMENT

LEADERSHIP VALUES

Blood relationship may have no bearing on what defines a family.

THE THIRD BATTALION FAMILY BIDS FOND FAREWELL TO CAPTAIN TOMMY ROCKE. (FRONT ROW WITH SUNGLASSES) UPON HIS RETIREMENT, JANUARY 2005.

PHOTO COURTESY OF THE PHILADELPHIA FIRE DEPARTMENT

THE MIGHTY 170 – A FAMILY FOREVER. 12/09/96 – 03/27/97

PHOTO COURTESY OF THE PHILADELPHIA FIRE DEPARTMENT

AN INTROSPECTION

Effective leaders care about all their family members.

NEWLY PROMOTED CLASS OF LIEUTENANTS AFTER
THEIR GRADUATION FROM THE PFD'S THREE-WEEK
OFFICER DEVELOPMENT CLASS, MARCH, 1996

PHOTO COURTESY OF THE PHILADELPHIA FIRE DEPARTMENT

INTROSPECTION

- Do you think that you score high in demonstrating the value of loyalty?

- Do you exhibit all the listed ten guide-point behaviors? Would all those around and under you agree with your assessment?

LEADERSHIP VALUES

- Are you actively cultivating loyalty in your team right now? How?

- Have you ever been in the center of one of those confusing, tug-of-war loyalty conflicts in which you were torn between two concerns, or two interests, or worse—two people? How did (and how do) you decide what to do? Does loyalty to yourself and to your core values ever enter your thought process?

- Is camaraderie on full display where you work? Who is most responsible for the current condition?

- Have you ever been unofficially warned or cautioned that an employee or team member was a loser or a problem child? Did you feel compelled to monitor that person's every single move with a magnifying glass, just anticipating and expecting a negative event? Did your actions become a self-fulfilling prophecy? Why?

- Do you view your work team as an extended family—and treat them as such?

CHAPTER 13

Humility

HUMILITY IS OUR CAPACITY FOR MODESTY; it's our sincere desire to be unpretentious. Leaders who possess humility have a realistic view of their own importance and do not regard themselves as more special or superior to other people. Humble leaders maintain a genuine sense of gratitude for all their blessings and freely offer deferential respect to other people. Displaying humility is not a sign of weakness; in fact, *The Economist* (2013) has called humility "the secret sauce" in outstanding leadership.

The difficulty in attempting to be a humble person is that inside all of us, leaders and followers alike, resides an incredibly powerful force—our ego. Our ego has both wonderful, positive potential and, if it gets out of control, disastrous, negative potential.

The human ego's potential for destruction is a powerful force that can propel and control our lives if we let it dominate our actions. Two important leadership questions then are:

- How do we make our ego work *for* us, and not *against* us?
- How do we subdue our ego and keep under control that part of us that needlessly complicates both our careers and personal lives—and manages to turn off so many people around us?

Because everyone, even our greatest leaders, are all human and imperfect, many of us struggle with this internal force that's continually attempting to bring us harm. Ego-induced damage can emerge in at least two different ways.

In the first harmful scenario, our ego causes us to continuously criticize, lash out at, or tear down other people. Jim Rohn, one of America's foremost business philosophers, clarifies for us that there are only two ways in which you can have "the tallest building in town." You can spend your time tearing down everyone else's buildings; or, you can keep working on improving and raising the height of your own. Your choice then becomes to be either a "wrecker" or a "builder."

In a second equally negative scenario, our ego is constantly striving to make us look more special, more gifted, and better than we truly are. How sad this is, as most of us already have so many wonderful talents and blessings. There is really no need to exaggerate.

When your ego seizes firm control of your personality, *everything*, as you see it, becomes all about you. It's your world, and everybody else in it is just a bit player. When you believe that the world revolves around you, you're always the main attraction. You're the star of the show yesterday, today, and for the foreseeable future.

AN INTROSPECTION

And, if you happen to be in a leadership position, an overblown ego just magnifies the negative outcomes. C'mon, think about it, we know that you're in charge of the Mid-Atlantic sales region, or the shop foreman, or the hospital's ICU supervisor; but, you gotta get a grip! How important can you really be? I mean *really*. There are over seven and a half billion people in the world ... 7 1/2 *billion*!

Sometimes leaders become so ego-centric that they forget one inevitable law of physics and nature: that everything we see or experience here on earth will one day return to "quiet dust" (Dyer, 1998). All elements of our physical universe are composed of matter and eventually that matter gets recycled to quiet dust. Everything. Even if it takes a million years. And, everything includes the pyramids, your classic Chevy, your long-awaited Final Report, your two-year projection on company growth strategies, and obviously our bodies. *Everything* on the planet has its own life cycle—and then it returns to quiet dust.

Wow! That sounds pretty bleak. Am I therefore saying that nothing matters; that *we* don't matter? On the contrary, I'm saying just the opposite: that every last one of us matters. But because it's the role of our leaders to sometimes dictate to others exactly what matters most, leaders must attempt to keep events and issues in perspective and balance. Without question, our most effective leaders incorporate both perspective and balance while leading their teams.

My career has unfortunately involved working for leaders who believed and acted like the world revolved around them. As such, we, "the lowly workers," had no true value. What a turn-off their poor

LEADERSHIP VALUES

leadership behavior was. It was clear that they felt that my colleagues and I had zero standing, relevance, or value in their world. So, guess what I did in my earlier years? I governed myself accordingly. To the degree possible, I just quietly "disconnected." Sadly, upon my disconnect, we *all* lost; the leader... me... and even the organization. Maybe you've been there?

Don't you find it interesting that some of our greatest lessons learned in work, and in life, come from bad people? Their actions clearly show us what NOT to do and what NOT to say. Our learning methodology is simply to observe their behavior... and do the opposite.

Bad experiences are a reality that we all have to endure. But, the biggest mistake is not to see, understand—and *learn from*—any lesson that the experience holds for us.

Believe me, it is still a constant struggle to keep my ego under control. With Wayne Dyer's help in *Wisdom of the Ages*, here are some lessons that I learned along the way:

- Make an effort to evaluate your words *before* you speak. If necessary, count to ten; then ask yourself whether the words you plan to say will really help the situation.
- Consciously cut down on the use of the words "I" and "Me" in your sentences. Think, and more importantly, sincerely *act* more in terms of "We" and "Us." When you're moving toward "We and Us Thinking" your capacity for leadership is growing.

AN INTROSPECTION

- Regularly practice silence. Try this change of pace, especially if you're an ego-driven leader: just shut up for a while. Let others have a platform while you just listen, evaluate, and think. Amazingly, some of the times that I felt most in control were the times I relinquished control.
- Understand humility. Having humility does not mean that you deny your power, talents, or special gifts; that would make you a phony. Rather, it means that you understand that your power, talents, and special gifts, at least to some degree, flow *through* you—not *from* you.
- Value humility; seek it, cultivate it, and practice it. A favorite related Chinese proverb of mine from Lao Tzu goes: "All streams flow to the ocean because the ocean is lower than they are; it is its humility that gives the ocean its power."
- Recognize the awesome power of your ego, and if you think it's hurting you in any way: confront it! Challenge all its negative dimensions. And, don't be surprised if attempting to subdue your ego turns out to be one of the toughest fights of your life. Many leaders engage in a lifelong battle struggling to keep their ego under control—against the worthiest of opponents. Every time you think that you have finally whipped your ego, it keeps getting up off the mat to challenge you and complicate your life. If you truly understand its potential negative power and consequences, you'll

appreciate how it can stand in the way of a wide range of potential successes that you could otherwise have.
- If you can, reduce, or even STOP, your ego's desperate need for attention. Stop making everything about you. Because if you can pull this off, it will be a giant step toward unlocking your very best self.

Unfortunately, humility is a lesson that many people must keep relearning. It can be extremely frustrating to purposely lead several "good" months in an unpretentious manner, being grateful for all your blessings, and treating everyone with respect and dignity—only to have it all evaporate in one brief, ugly, ego-driven act. But, don't give up. Conquering the dark side of your ego is always a battle worth fighting.

It helps me to remember that the primary leadership goal must be to do the right things—for the right reasons. If I'm acting inappropriately because of my ego-driven need for attention, compliments, praise, glory, or applause, I know that my leadership foundation will be much too feeble to successfully withstand the inevitable challenges.

One of my strongest, personal "Leadership #101 Truisms" is that: "People only *willingly* follow those who they respect, and, they are not going to willingly follow anyone who does not respect *them!*" Isn't this true?

AN INTROSPECTION

TOO BIG FOR MY BRITCHES

I recall the morning I received a call from Car 2's secretary while I was commanding Engine 24. She instructed me to report to Deputy Commissioner Kite's office in Headquarters the next day at 10 AM in full dress uniform, and didn't provide any reason for the order. I was alarmed and confused; to my knowledge, everything had been going great at 24's. I called my battalion chief and asked if he could shed any light on the order; he knew nothing.

Later that afternoon, I called a friend who was assigned to the Department's Research and Planning Unit. I persuaded him to tell me off the record that the Department was only about a month away from opening its newly-constructed second fire station at the Philadelphia International Airport. I had been selected to be the first commanding officer of the brand-new crash crew station: Engine 78.

This was horrible news for me. I didn't want to go anywhere. I loved 24's, the station, and all the guys. I was so upset.

The next morning, Harry Kite, the elderly well-respected Deputy Commissioner, beckoned me into his office and motioned for me to sit in front of him. He opened with a few nice remarks about my performance at 24's and then told me that they were transferring me to Engine 78 effective 8 AM, Monday morning.

LEADERSHIP VALUES

"So, Cap, what do you think?" he asked with a broad smile on his weathered face.

"I think it stinks, Commissioner. I feel like I'm being punished for doing a good job at 24's. I don't want to go down there and work with those guys. Most of them are just looking to get out of fire duty, coasting through their careers, or counting their days until pension. I prefer to stay right where I am; you just said that I'm doing a good job. Besides, for me, this job is all about fire duty."

Immediately, the broad smile vanished from his face. "Are you serious?" he asked.

"Absolutely. I don't want to go there. I'm a firefighter, Commissioner, I want to serve in the busiest stations, in the worst neighborhoods, for as long as I can."

Now he sat more erect behind the large oak desk. "Do you know what I wish, Cap? I wish all those people who recommended you for this assignment were here to witness this. Trust me, I had other captains in mind; but people kept telling me that you were the best person for this job. I think they would all be shocked at your reaction."

"I'm sorry, Commissioner, I just don't want to go there. I think that I can be much more valuable to the Department by staying at 24's."

"Listen to yourself. Do you ever utter any sentences that don't have the words I or me in it?"

AN INTROSPECTION

"Commissioner, I understand that you're disappointed. If you have to, transfer me to the officer pool. At least I'll still be involved in active firefighting."

With the sternest of tones, he let me have it, "Oh, I'm going to transfer you alright. But it won't be to the pool. Don't you understand what's happening here? The Department has selected you for a once-in-a-lifetime assignment. It's an incredible opportunity for you; there's never been an Engine 78. You'll be in on the ground-floor, creating and building a vital unit that is desperately needed to ensure regional public safety. Are you afraid of the challenge?"

I didn't say anything.

"You know, ever since you sat down, all I've heard is *your* wants, *your* wishes. This isn't about you; it's about you being part of our team. To me, you just look like a selfish kid with an enormous ego who cares nothing about the needs of the organization. You really have an inflated opinion of your own value to the Department. Oh, you're fine when things are going your way—a full tour of duty at 68's, a first command assignment at 24's. But the minute the organization needs a commitment from *you*—you selfishly run away." I felt crushing embarrassment; he was right.

He paused for a deep breath and continued in on me hard, "I think this whole firefighting service requirement of yours is total bullshit. I read your file. A year at 60's, then to Ladder 24

LEADERSHIP VALUES

to 16's to three years at 68's and now the captain of 24's. Do you understand that you're seeing the *same* type of fires over and over again? They're just in different sections of the city. Don't you have the strategies and tactics down by now? Do you think that you're still learning and growing every day as much as you could—or *should*? With 78's, I'm offering you something so different, so special, and so unique, and you can't—or won't—think about anybody other than yourself. I personally don't know what all these people see in you."

Those last comments hurt me deeply; it was now clear that I was letting down more people than Commissioner Kite. It felt like he'd stuck a dagger in my heart—and slowly twisted it in all directions while he looked me in the eyes. Then it got worse; he got visibly angry and raised his voice.

"So, let me be really clear here, Captain. I'm positively transferring you to Engine 78. What we're talking about here? All this crap you're handing me today? This is now about whether you're going to the airport as a demoted platoon lieutenant or the commanding officer. You got me?"

Commissioner Kite didn't let up, "It's your choice how you want to walk through that front door of 78's when it opens. Take tonight and think about it long and hard, because this is a career-defining moment for you. Call me at 9 AM tomorrow morning and tell me your decision; do you want to report in as the captain or just a platoon lieutenant? Now, get out of my sight."

AN INTROSPECTION

I didn't sleep at all that night; I just kept reliving those embarrassing, painful fifteen minutes in his office. Everything he said was true; I placed my needs and desires above those of the Department.

Of course, I called at 8:55 AM the next morning. I told the Deputy Commissioner that I would go willingly to 78's and do the very best job I could for as long as required.

I had hoped that he would say something about regretting being so tough on me, that he knew I'd do a great job, and that he wished me a ton of luck. It never happened. He was off the phone in five seconds with, "Okay, the transfer will be out Friday. Don't let us down!"

I deserved every bit of his curt response. I had clearly demonstrated not only my professional immaturity, but a deep love of self that was boosted by an ugly, inflated ego.

Commissioner Kite was right about another thing too: the next several weeks were among the most interesting that I would ever get to spend in my entire career. The tasks were certainly challenging, and I was forced way out of my comfort zone, but everything that Commissioner Kite alluded to came to fruition. I was present and had valued input at every important meeting concerning the opening of the station. And it wasn't only at fire department meetings; I attended vital sessions with the Division of Aviation, the Commerce Department, Fleet Management, and the Federal Aviation Administration. My days started early and ended very late.

LEADERSHIP VALUES

I was also delighted that the officers and firefighters of Engine 77—the existing airport crash-crew—would drive over at a moment's notice to help me with cleaning, furniture deliveries, vehicle delivery and testing, and anything else I needed. And they always came with genuine smiles on their faces, ready to do anything I asked. I felt silent embarrassment of my previous opinion of them.

Late one Saturday afternoon, nine days before the official "Going in Service" date, I was working in civilian clothes in the watch desk/lobby area of 78's when I saw a huge red Cadillac convertible pull into the station parking lot. Out stepped a fiftyish, roly-poly gentleman who immediately went to his car trunk. After retrieving a large gym bag and a suitcase, he approached the station front door. Newly assigned firefighters were not scheduled to report-in until the next week, but it was clear to me that he was the first arrival of my new team. I held the door for him as he wrestled the large suitcase into the watch desk area.

"How ya' doin', pal. I'm Al Boghosian. Maybe you heard of me, most people call me 'Big Al.' I was down this way, so I thought I'd give it a shot in dropping my stuff off."

"No problem," I said, "want me to show you to your personal locker and where to stow your running gear?"

"That'd be great."

I had heard Al's name a lot, but, I never worked with him. He had a reputation for being an accomplished schmoozer, a

AN INTROSPECTION

masterful cadger, and a splendid salesman for PFD Thrill Show Tickets and other departmental charitable events. No one ever mentioned if he could fight fires; maybe no one knew. It didn't matter; I knew that I would require at least one of these types of individuals on my station team.

After stowing all his items, including the big personal pillow from his suitcase, I asked him if he would like a brief tour of the station.

His eyes lit up, "Absolutely."

After my narrated fifteen-minute walk-around, I could see that he was very impressed. Who wouldn't be? The brand-new station and apparatus were spectacular.

As I escorted Al to the front door, he proclaimed, "Yeah, I think I'm gonna like it here. The only thing I'm concerned about is our captain. I hear this Appleby's a real pistol and pissed off at coming here. You know this guy can make our lives miserable. If he's unhappy, he might spend every day breaking our balls. What do you think?"

I replied, "I think the captain has experienced a career-changing event. He will be coming here full of humility and ready to keep an open mind toward everything—and everybody." I meant those words.

We walked out together to his car. Al opened the door of his luxurious Caddy and eased himself into the soft white leather seat. Gently, I pushed the door closed for him.

LEADERSHIP VALUES

"By the way," he said, "I never did get your name. Are we going to be working the same platoon together?"

"No, Al. I'm working the 'D' platoon. My name is Appleby."

Like he received an electric shock, he suddenly jerked his head and stared straight ahead. In three or four seconds, he turned to face me again and said, "Someday this will be a great story, Cap." Then he burst out laughing—and I did too.

So, what have I learned about humility's connection to leadership? Well, I know that not all leaders among us arrive with a sense of innate humility. I learned that this lack of humility frequently complicates their efforts to connect with and lead their teams. It's just not that much fun or gratifying working for (or with) selfish, self-absorbed blowhards who are incapable of assuming or understanding any perspective other than their own.

I also learned that most leaders who struggle to attain and hold onto genuine humility require periodic gentle reminders—or even a well-timed kick in the butt—to rein in their egos. As a leader, I've therefore learned to be grateful for all those gentle, or even the not-so-gentle, reminders to keep my ego under control. I consider those reminders to be priceless personal "tutoring sessions" handed down from above—to never again let me get too big for my britches.

AN INTROSPECTION

New Firehouse Open at Airport

A new $400,000-firehouse was put into service yesterday at International Airport to increase fire protection there, Fire Commissioner Joseph R. Rizzo announced.

The new station, an 11,000-square-foot building designed by Thomas Mangan of Fort Washington, is located on Island Rd. adjacent to the Overseas Terminal.

FROM THE *PHILADELPHIA DAILY NEWS*, DECEMBER 9, 1975

During my twenty-five-month tour-of-duty as a crash crew commanding officer, I experienced first-hand the trauma and emotion of *three* aircraft crashes. I thought back to Chief Kite's promise of a once-in-a-lifetime experience. He was right; it was. And, I remain grateful. On a lighter note: After my third crash, a high-ranking chief at Headquarters suggested that I was somehow a jinx. He said, "We better get Appleby out of there. These planes are falling out of the sky on us!"

LEADERSHIP VALUES

PHOTO COURTESY OF THE PHILADELPHIA FIRE DEPARTMENT

103 on Jet Hurt In Airport Crash
Death Cheated in Freak Crash
Airliner Crashes Trying to Land In Storm at Airport

FROM THE *PHILADELPHIA DAILY NEWS* AND *THE PHILADELPHIA INQUIRER*, 103 PEOPLE ABOARD—EVERYONE SURVIVED.
JUNE 23, 1976

AN INTROSPECTION

JANUARY 11, 1977. CAPTAIN APPLEBY (LEFT) DISCUSSING ISSUES WITH DEPUTY CHIEF PETE BLACK FOLLOWING THE CRASH LANDING OF A TWIN-ENGINE AIRCRAFT. ALL EIGHT PEOPLE ABOARD SURVIVED.

PHOTO COURTESY OF THE PHILADELPHIA FIRE DEPARTMENT

JUNE 20, 1977. ALL THREE PEOPLE ABOARD THIS SINGLE-ENGINE AIRCRAFT SURVIVED THE CRASH.

PHOTO COURTESY OF THE PHILADELPHIA FIRE DEPARTMENT

LEADERSHIP VALUES

INTROSPECTION

- How would you rate yourself on humility? Would most people say that you are sincerely humble?

- In an honest reflection, do you spend any time tearing down other peoples' buildings or aggressively acting as your own press agent? Do you think others notice that about you?

- In your leadership role, do you spend more time boasting and bragging about yourself—or commending the actions of others?

- On those occasions when you do something nice for someone, how important is it that you receive positive feedback or praise? Are you upset when it doesn't come?

- Do you still remember *and appreciate* all the breaks and good fortune that came your way? How do you show that appreciation?

- Do you pay much more attention to the words and ideas of your boss than to your peers and subordinates? Is there ever any occasion in which their words or ideas might be more important than those of your boss?

CHAPTER 14

Enlightenment

BECAUSE ENLIGHTENMENT COMES IN THOUSANDS OF FORMS and there is no single universal agreement of its definition or description, I can't be as straightforward in addressing this final leadership value as I was with the previous thirteen. As imprecise as it is, I still want to share some thoughts on my experiences with enlightened leaders. I will attempt to define enlightenment, suggest how one might acquire it, and describe how my enlightened leaders acted.

WHAT IS ENLIGHTENMENT?

While there's no definitive definition, I can tell you that enlightenment is not what I initially thought it was—an attainment of some heightened mystical sense of awareness. I thought that if I was "enlightened," I would proceed through life in some type of a Zen state. People would overhear me chanting mystically from the firehouse bunkroom while wearing a multi-colored robe and a peculiar hat, or watch me "communicating" with trees on the firehouse lawn. Of course, I was wrong about this notion. True enlightenment can be as simple as having some "awakening experiences" that cause your previous assumptions or belief paradigms to change (maybe even burst) by some new (maybe profound?) realizations (Dyer, 1998).

Are you familiar with the Zen proverb: *"Before enlightenment, chopping wood, carrying water. After enlightenment, chopping wood, carrying water"*? I believe that it's worth thinking about from a leadership perspective. If you contemplate the proverb's message, you see that it means that the world does not change around you when you become enlightened. It can't; the world must go on—regardless. In work, there are always going to be:

- Clueless leaders.
- Mountains of paperwork and red tape.
- Umpteen layers of bureaucracy to get something done.
- Endless and sometimes insane hoops that you must jump through just to keep moving forward.
- All the other voluminous barriers and impediments that disappoint and frustrate you on a regular basis.

You see, you'll *always* have to be chopping wood and carrying water. That's the "way of the world"—and you're part of the world. Because of this, *real* change is going to have to come from within you. The enlightened change happens when you begin viewing the world with new eyes. Observing events from a different view leads to a new attitude.

AN INTROSPECTION

HOW DO YOU BECOME ENLIGHTENED?

One way to achieve enlightenment is to begin viewing life's events though a different lens, since a new view can lead to a new attitude. You're still you; only now, you *choose* to put on different "glasses" to see everything. Looking through these new glasses changes your attitude toward everything that life throws at you.

This change is most noticeable in that you choose to be immersed in a personal inner peace or calmness. This serenity is most evident in challenging times, when all those around you are "spazzing out."

Of course, the fact that this new outlook is toning you down a bit doesn't mean that you become indifferent to these events—especially if you're the leader and you're accountable. It just means knowing that *you have the power to choose* your personal "button-pushing" events and keep them to a minimum. More simply said: a huge part of enlightenment is understanding what is truly important in your career—and in your life—and choosing to use that focus as a daily guide. And it involves remembering that:

- Not every fire must be a life-threatening, spectacular extra alarm.
- Not every disagreement must escalate to the level of a steel cage match.
- Not every subpoena must send you running to the bathroom.
- Not every work assignment must take a severe toll on your physical, mental, and emotional wellness.

When you attempt to become an enlightened leader, you are constantly choosing not to let things get to you, whatever they are—but especially inconsequential events.

When you're truly enlightened, you try very hard to make sure that no *thing*—or no *person*—can push your buttons. When I start getting upset because someone is pushing an "Appleby button," I try to remember at that particular moment that this person is, in a very weird way, actually doing me a favor by reminding me that I have not yet mastered myself. I'm still not in total 100 percent control of my emotions.

It's disappointing that after all these years, I'm still a work in progress. The only good news is that I am able to see the "finished product" with 20/20 vision. And being able to see my best possible self often helps to guide me toward better control and a better outcome.

WHAT DOES ENLIGHTENED LEADERSHIP BEHAVIOR LOOK LIKE?

Over my career, I noticed that the truly special leaders I encountered seemed to be on a different spatial plane than me; that is, they seemed to have a different "intake prism" than I did. We didn't process things in the same way.

We would both witness the identical event, sometimes catastrophic, but they saw something that I didn't see. We both were in the same meeting, yet they took away a different message than I did. We both read the same document, yet they predicted a completely different result than I did.

AN INTROSPECTION

I believe what these unique leaders had that I lacked was enlightenment. They had their "special filter glasses" on that provided them with a different attitude than I had. I wish that I had a better word for their intangible quality, but I can't come up with one. So, I'm staying with enlightenment. However, I do think that the word fits because true enlightenment comes from true wisdom, and all these leaders possessed true wisdom. They all had an extraordinary understanding of three things:

- What was true.
- What was right.
- What was lasting.

And the source of this understanding did not just come from a book, or a seminar, or even from a formal course on philosophy or leadership. It came in large part from their personal values; they were actually trying to *live* what was really important to them.

Specifically, what separated me from these enlightened leaders was the aforementioned *attitude* they possessed. Our different attitudes produced our different intake systems. And I noticed five describable behaviors that I witnessed from my enlightened leaders.

The very first thing that one of these enlightened leaders would do when something went wrong was to always seek initially to understand and never to blame. His or her innate reflex action was always, "*Why* did this happen?"—not the customary, "Who screwed this up? Give me a name!" None of the enlightened leaders that I observed ever wasted precious time at the beginning of a problem attempting to place blame or find fault. Instead, it usually went like this: "OK, something is wrong; it negatively affects the team, the mission, or the vision and I'm going to devote *all* of my energy to fixing the problem. Any required straightening out of people can certainly come later." For the enlightened leader, assessing and assigning blame was not an immediate priority.

Secondly, the enlightened leader would always reflect inward and look *at himself (or herself)*, either quietly as if checking some type of an internal mirror, or sometimes even publicly, right in front of us. The leader would honestly and brutally assess his/her own actions, behavior, or contribution to the situation. They sincerely sought to know whether *they* had any responsibility, whether large or small, in causing the dilemma at hand: "Gary, maybe it's not his fault. Maybe this happened because *we* didn't provide enough of the right training."

Thirdly, I noticed that occasionally, the enlightened leaders would refrain from fully engaging in an event, choosing instead to take on the role of "observer"—looking in from the outside and drinking in all the turmoil around the situation. I sensed the leaders' disappointment in recognizing that all the accompanying emotion was actually a huge distraction. My enlightened leaders knew that the theatrics surrounding the event were just human beings being human. When we were posturing, and venting, and acting angry, selfish, scared, petty, small-minded, ego-centric, or just plain weak, the leaders recognized that there was a large, needless emotional "game" going on over and above the legitimate problem at hand. And the enlightened leaders simply refused to get sucked into the "emotional vortex" to which their

AN INTROSPECTION

team members had fallen victim. Instead, they *chose* to save all their energy for actually resolving the problem.

Fourth, even though they were unquestionably decisive leaders, on certain occasions, the enlightened ones were clearly slower than the rest of us to make assumptions about situations and especially assumptions about people. They just seemed to sense which situations required them to let things play out for a while. In these moments, they were less likely to arrive at a snap conclusion, especially based on a singular event. Consequently, many times, the "enlightened ones" could be identified as the only ones with no egg on their faces. They demonstrated for me how we humans—especially when serving as leaders—can significantly uncomplicate our lives if we just cut down our rapid rate of daily assumptions and snap decisions.

Fifth and finally, these leaders were always paying serious attention to the "connection" that is supposed to exist between a leader and his/her followers. Do you think that every leader grasps the enormity of what happened to him/her on promotion day? When you are designated as a leader, you are put in charge of a piece of the organization's most valuable resource—its "intellectual capital" (Stewart, 1998). In every office, warehouse, school, work site, etc., at 8 o'clock in the morning and 5 o'clock in the evening (or thereabouts), every day, the most important organizational components, the *real* inventory, comes to work and goes home. Enlightened leaders understand this and they instinctively focus primarily on the organization's real inventory—*its people*! Consequently, these enlightened leaders pay consistent attention to all their relationships.

LEADERSHIP VALUES

Looking back at these five qualities or behaviors, I eventually came to understand what was actually occurring right in front of me: my leader was exhibiting enlightenment. He or she was focusing on what his/her personal values indicated was true, right, and lasting. If you can learn to make yourself focus like this, even a little bit, it will certainly help you to separate the nonsense from the truly important issues.

The good news for me (hopefully for you too) is that I have found that enlightenment opportunities pop up frequently. Many of them emanate from the most unexpected sources and at the most unusual times. You simply have to remain open and ready to at least consider a thought or idea that differs from your established assumptions and beliefs. And, of course, you must be astute enough to recognize the valuable wisdom in what you just saw, read, heard or experienced.

One personal example of an enlightenment opportunity that I was lucky enough to recognize took place many years ago. During an interview, actress/singer Cher was discussing the positive influence that her mother's advice had on her while growing up, and said that her mother told her, "If it doesn't matter in five years, it doesn't matter."

I started thinking deeply about that insight and realized that it had application for me too. Because, so often, I would be hopping mad or upset at something or someone and then remember the point that Cher's mother made. And, then I would realize—*Five years? Wow! I won't even remember this event clearly five weeks from now! I have to back off... calm down... and let it go.* Her enlightenment "jewel" has become one of my most consistent go-to strategies to cope with some of life's more unpleasant moments.

AN INTROSPECTION

The strategy works. And, I pass the jewel on to you as my gift. Use it; in both your personal and professional life. That's about as close as I can come to be a Zen Master.

THE FIREBOMBING

Remembering back to that night at Engine #31 as a brand-new lieutenant:

It's around three o'clock in the morning and we're responding first-due to a reported house fire. Approaching a block of two-story row homes, most with outdoor porches, I can see flames pouring out of a first-floor living room window, across the wooden porch, and almost out to the sidewalk area. Someone had thrown a Molotov cocktail through the home's first-floor window.

I knew that the appropriate firefighting tactic was for our first pumper (called the "Wagon") to stop momentarily at a hydrant close to the fire, wrap the 2 ½" hoseline around it, and lead in "on the fly." However, I was so excited that I couldn't verbalize the order to my pumper driver. In my hyped-up state, the words just wouldn't come out. The pumper driver pulled in to the hydrant anyway and one firefighter jumped off with the equipment, completed the wrap-around, banged on the cab and yelled, "Okay!" We were off in a split-second, approaching the fire with my heart about to leap out of my chest. This was going to be my first "good job" as an officer.

LEADERSHIP VALUES

Pulling close to the fire, I wanted to make sure that my crew chose to attack the fire with a 1½" hoseline rather than selecting the 1" booster line which was a dangerous, but often-used, tactic back then. I gave a brief report on the radio and requested more assistance. When I exited the officer's front seat, my crew was already knocking down the exterior flames with our 1½" hoseline. I never got to order the size of the attack line.

Because of my crew's aggressiveness and courage, it seemed like only seconds passed before we were already advancing into the first-floor living room. Both floors of the entire structure were heavily involved in fire; you could smell the gasoline. Based on my West Philly experience, I knew that truly "Big Guys" always place a second hoseline in service.

But before I could order it, one member of my crew tapped me on the shoulder and said, "Hey, Loot, I'm going to get us another line so we can make the second floor."

And they did. My crew extinguished just about the entire body of fire on *both* floors. It was a stunningly competent piece of firefighting.

When the first chief officer arrived on the scene, he entered the smoldering first-floor where we were starting to overhaul with some other companies. Chief McGonigle took a long look at everything; you could sense that he was very impressed.

The chief asked, "Who's in charge of 31's?"

I said, "Me, Chief, Lieutenant Appleby from the Division Pool."

AN INTROSPECTION

He walked closer to me through the smoky haze, looked me up and down, and then said in a loud voice, "You did a great job here Lieutenant; you made a good stop."

"Thank you," I weakly replied.

I could see all of 31's crew members grinning at me. And then we all went back to work.

At the conclusion of the 8 AM formal roll call back at the station, one of 31's senior members said, "Hey, Lootie, let us know when you're coming back. You'll have to sit down and break bread with us; we'd like to get to know more about you. That is, of course, after you hold one of those damn training sessions."

They all broke out in laughter; but it was okay, because I smiled from ear-to-ear too. I knew then that we had both taken the measure of each other—and we both respected what we had seen. I drove home on Cloud Nine.

Over the next few days off-duty, I couldn't stop thinking about that fire. Everything had worked out perfectly; but I knew that *I* hadn't given one single order. Whether I was in charge that morning or not, 31's was still going to perform in the same outstanding fashion. There could have been a sack of potatoes in the officer's seat and that fire still would have been extinguished expediently and professionally. Would all my studies and preparation on how to lead go out the window? I had to figure it out: *Exactly where do I fit in? Exactly when do I (should I) get to perform this leadership thing?*

LEADERSHIP VALUES

So, what was the life-long leadership enlightenment lesson that the firebombing job taught me? Namely this: effective, credible leadership does not have to include personally supervising every single aspect of my team's activities. I'm going to be needed *most* when the direction to go in is gray—or worse yet, black, or any shade in between. As the leader, I must be the one who is always shining "the light."

Through 31's actions, I felt enlightened. It was like I had accidentally discovered the key to some secret leadership treasure vault. I understood and accepted that there will be plenty of opportunities for me to demonstrate genuine active leadership through a wide variety of ways other than micromanaging. I can lead by living my vision, being a role model, inspiring, motivating, helping, and guiding my team, and in dozens of other important ways in scenarios I hadn't even imagined yet. But I did not have to micromanage.

Because I had been micromanaged as a firefighter at 16's, I totally understood that it is a leadership killer. When I was assigned to Engine 16 under "Captain Straight Arrow," our entire company felt frustrated, demoralized, and disempowered. Our "leader" could not let go of his extraordinary concern with minutiae or tiny details. His actions were so blatant that the rest of the Eleventh Battalion referred to our station as "Stalag 16" (a term used for WWII German prisoner-of-war camps).

AN INTROSPECTION

Straight Arrow's effect on our team was devastating. His lack of leadership damaged our confidence, hurt our performance, and hampered us from growing or developing. Any positive results that he did receive from micromanaging were only short-term; he had zero concern about the "big picture." As for his vision—he never articulated one. He was too busy micromanaging our every move.

I bet that you too worked for a micromanager at one time in your career. Can you remember how suffocating it feels to be micromanaged?

So, if you're a leader who is currently applying the same level of scrutiny, intensity, and an in-your-face oversight approach to *every* task—please consider stepping back. Try using a little more of the "What" not "How" approach toward achieving success in directing your team's activities. Personally, if I was a little unsure of obtaining compliance, I would just give my team more detail on the "What"—and still leave the "How" up to them. I promise that moving away from micromanaging will be a significant, enlightened move toward *real* leadership.

LEADERSHIP VALUES

ENGINE #31 AND BATTALION CHIEF #6 IN THE MID-1970s

PHOTO COURTESY OF FIREMAN'S HALL MUSEUM, PHILADELPHIA

INTROSPECTION

- Where are you on the journey to enlightenment?

- When things go wrong, do you ever examine your own role or contribution first?

- When you're faced with a problem, do you focus all your available energy on resolving the issue—or do you usually get sucked in to playing those emotional "people games"?

- How would you rate your snap decision reflexes? Slow? Medium? Like a rocket? How often are you wrong?

- In work, what are your leadership priorities? Are they even remotely connected to what is true, what is right, and what is lasting?

- Are you truly open to any awakening experiences? How do you know that?

- Can you acknowledge a genuine moment of enlightenment that you've had in the last several years—a moment that provided you with a piece of true, everlasting wisdom?

LEADERSHIP VALUES

- Can you be dirt-ball honest with yourself? What if you worked *for you*? Would you be thrilled and grateful to work for you? Or, after digesting these chapters and stories, did a picture start to emerge in which you realize that maybe you're no box of chocolates to work for after all? Is it too late for you to change?

Epilogue

HERE IS YOUR LONE FINAL EXAM QUESTION. If you understood the main theme of my fourteen leadership values, the answer may be obvious. What was *Leadership Values: An Introspection* all about?

One way, among many, to become a better leader is to become a better "_____." What? Any guesses?

Become a better **person**! It seems pretty clear to me, and hopefully by now, to you as well, that we can sum up all my thoughts, lessons, and stories with this one point. How can you be a truly good leader—if you're not a good person with good values? Values that, at the minimum, I recommend include:

- INTEGRITY
- VISION
- DECISIVENESS
- SELF-DISCIPLINE
- ACCOUNTABILITY
- OPTIMISM
- COURAGE
- HONESTY
- TRUSTWORTHINESS
- PRIDE
- COMPASSION
- LOYALTY
- HUMILITY
- ENLIGHTENMENT

LEADERSHIP VALUES

So, what a good place this is for you to begin or renew your quest for outstanding leadership. Begin by leading *yourself*. If need be, lead yourself through an introspection, to a better you!

By examining all these leadership values, or a different selection of your choice, you can see all the choices that lie in front of you. And I assure you that they will be choices; for your organization's ability to mold you into a desired form is limited. It really is.

In the end, it will come down to the *choices* that you make, and especially, the difficult choices; the ones that keep you awake at night and weigh heavy on your mind and your heart. Those are the choices that will actually define your character, as well as the true effectiveness and quality of your leadership. So, the decision will be yours. What will you be about? What will your leadership legacy be?

Professional and workplace legacies can be tricky things. We're creating our own legacy day after day, week after week, year after year, but most of us aren't really paying attention. Then one day, you transfer, quit, or retire, and you realize that you left behind a legacy by which the whole organization, unit, or team will remember you.

Sometimes, people have regrets. Some leaders look back and wish they had created and handed down a better legacy. They realize that they didn't leave the best part of them "selves" for others to remember them by. They failed to inspire anyone by the example they set, and are pretty sure others won't remember their ideas, experiences, achievements, friendship, values, or good deeds. As leaders, they had both the control and the opportunity to shape a positive legacy—but

AN INTROSPECTION

they blew it. They provided zero meaningful, enduring impact that could have helped others in leading their lives.

There are no laws mandating that you consciously work to create a legacy. That thought doesn't even occur to many wonderful, talented leaders who do leave shining legacies. But legacies are left no matter what we do—or don't do. The undeniable fact is that people *are* going to remember you in some fashion, whether they say:

- "She was the greatest! Never once did I doubt that she truly cared about all of us."
- "We didn't have much interaction. He was okay; he just came to work, did his job, and then went home. He never said much to anyone."
- "He was a useless bum. Every paycheck he ever drew from the organization was stolen money."

Creating your legacy is not that complex; the creation lies mostly in your actions or inactions, based largely on living your personal values system.

LEADERSHIP VALUES

Your Leadership Legacy?

Look at the flags: reflect on those or other positive values. Are they the legacy you are currently building?

You *are* going to be remembered; *how* you are remembered is mostly up to you.

Acknowledgments

Most especially to Teresa...
and to

Jil, Lauren, Cate, Abby, Sean, Bill, Mom, and Uncle Pat for constantly inspiring me and reminding me of the truly important things in life...

my three brothers—Fran, Tom and Ted—whose values and friendship have fed my spirit for a lifetime...

all the "Sixtieth Streeters" from Southwest Philly whose positive values infused my mind, my heart, and my soul—to this day...

and a special *Thank You* to those who played an important role in the publishing of this book: Bob Marchisello (Deputy Chief, Retired, PFD); Andrew Miller (M.A., Neumann University); Natasa Lekic and Christine Moore (New York Book Editors); and Tara Mayberry, (book designer, TeaberryCreative.com).

LEADERSHIP VALUES

* * *

All photographs, unless otherwise noted, are the property of the author.

Bibliography

Anderson, S. (n.d.). The 40-70 rule. Retrieved from http://integratedleader.com/articles/40-70rule.pdf

Ashford, S., & Detert, J. (2015, January/February). Get the boss to buy in. *Harvard Business Review.*

Barnes, L. (1981, March/April). Managing the paradox of organizational trust. *Harvard Business Review.*

Bartosz, B. (2001). *Tin helmets—Iron men: Philadelphia fires 50's-60's-70's.* Battle Ground, WA: Pediment.

Bennis, W. (1989). *On becoming a leader.* New York, NY: Perseus Publishing.

Bennis, W. (1996). Leadership for the 21st Century. *Visendus Seminar.*

Bennis, W., & Nanus, B. (1985). *Leaders: The strategies for taking charge.* New York, NY: Harper & Row.

Cheng, V. (2015, April 20). How to make impossible decisions. Retrieved from https://www.caseinterview.com

Covey, S. (1989). *The seven habits of highly effective people: Powerful lessons in personal change.* New York, NY: Simon & Schuster.

Dickinson, E. (2005). This quiet dust was gentlemen and ladies. In R. W. Franklin (Ed.), *The Poems of Emily Dickinson.* Cambridge, MA: Harvard University Press.

Dyer, W. (1998). *Wisdom of the ages: Sixty days to enlightenment.* New York, NY: HarperCollins.

Emerson, R. W. (1883). *Letters and social aims.* Boston, MA.

Fisher, R.-L. (2017). *The topography of tears.* New York, NY: Bellevue Literary Press.

French, W., & Bell, C. (1995). *Organization development: Behavioral science interventions for organization improvement.* Englewood Cliffs, NJ: Prentice Hall.

Harari, O. (1996). *Quotations from Chairman Powell: A leadership primer.* Retrieved from https://www.govleaders.org/powell.htm

How accountability leads to success. (2015, December 15). Retrieved from https://www.geteverwise.com

Hughes, T. (Producer), & Ebersole, P. D. (Director). (2013, May 6). *Dear Mom, Love Cher.* United States, Lifetime.

Jain, S. (2014, March 7). The importance of giving credit. *Harvard Business Review.*

Jones, E. (1908). Rationalization in every-day life. *The Journal of Abnormal Psychology,* 3(3), 161-169.

Kotter, J. (1996). *Leading change: An action plan from the world's foremost expert on business leadership.* Boston, MA: Harvard Business Review Press.

Kouzes, J., & Posner, B. (2011). *Credibility: How leaders gain it and lose it; Why people demand it.* San Francisco, CA: Jossey Bass.

Lue, N. (2014, May 12). Being loyal is a great quality—Don't mix it up with servitude. Retrieved from https://www.baggagereclaim.com

Lumsdaine, E., & Lumsdaine, M. (1995). *Creative problem solving: Thinking skills for a changing world.* New York, NY: McGraw-Hill.

Marchisello, R. (2017). *A firefighter's journal: Thirty-seven years on the firegrounds and in the firehouses of Philadelphia.* Philadelphia, PA: Robert J. Marchisello.

Nanus, B. (1989). *The leader's edge: The seven keys to leadership in a turbulent world.* Chicago, IL: Contemporary Books.

Nanus, B. (1995). *Visionary leadership.* New York, NY: John Wiley & Sons.

Orloff, J. (2004). *Positive energy: Ten extraordinary prescriptions for transforming fatigue, stress and fear into vibrance, strength, and love.* New York, NY: Three Rivers Press.

Peoples, D. (1992). *Presentations plus: David Peoples' proven techniques.* New York, NY: John Wiley & Sons.

Peters, T., & Waterman, R. (1982). *In search of excellence: Lessons from America's best-run companies.* New York, NY: Harper & Row.

Powell, C. (2012). *It worked for me: In life and leadership.* New York, NY: HarperCollins.

Richmond, W. (2007). *What I've learned: Thoughts from a fire chief.* Bloomington, IN: iUniverse.

Rothwell, W., & Kazanas, H. (1992). *Mastering the instructional design process: A systematic approach.* San Francisco, CA: Jossey Bass.

Scott, C., Jaffe, D., & Tobe, G. (1993). *Organizational vision, values and mission: Building the organization of tomorrow.* Menlo Park, CA: Crisp Publications.

Senge, P. (1990). *The fifth discipline: The art and practice of the learning organization.* New York, NY: Doubleday.

Shah, D. (2013, July 23). Seven qualities of a truly loyal employee. Retrieved from https://www.linkedin.com

Shaw, R. (1997). *Trust in the balance: Building successful organizations on results, integrity and concern.* San Francisco, CA: Jossey Bass.

Smith, J. (2002). *Strategic and tactical considerations on the fireground.* Upper Saddle River, NJ: Prentice Hall.

Stewart, T. (1997). *Intellectual capital: The new wealth of organizations.* New York, NY: Doubleday.

Swaine, Z. (2017, October 2). Colin Powell's 40-70 Approach to leadership and executive decisions. Retrieved from https://www.fa-mag.com/fa-online/news

The 125th Anniversary Book Committee. (1999). *Hike out: The history of the Philadelphia Fire Department.* Philadelphia, PA: Philadelphia Fire Department Historical Corporation.

Treasurer, B. (2016, April 28). Stupid courage vs. smart courage. Retrieved from https://www.linkedin.com

Useem, M. (1998). *The leadership moment: Nine true stories of triumph and disaster and their lessons for us all.* New York, NY: Three Rivers Press.

Wilcox, E. (1883). *Solitude.* Retrieved from https://www.familyfriendpoems.com

Wright, J. (2018). *From horses to horsepower: A history of Philadelphia's fire apparatus 1871 to 2017.* Battle Ground, WA: Pediment

About the Author

YOUNG FIREFIGHTER APPLEBY HELPING TO RESCUE A FALLEN COMRADE FOLLOWING A BUILDING COLLAPSE DURING A 1968 FOUR-ALARM FIRE IN WEST PHILADELPHIA.

PHOTO CREDIT – *THE PHILADELPHIA INQUIRER*

LEADERSHIP VALUES

Gary Appleby is a retired, forty-year veteran of the Philadelphia Fire Department. During his long career, Gary was promoted to every civil service rank and held the PFD's highest civil service rank of deputy chief for 25 years. His career included two years as a crash crew commanding officer at Philadelphia International Airport, three and a half years as the PFD's Executive Officer, and seven years serving as the Director of the Fire Academy. In 1998, Gary was a Fire Department Instructor's Conference (FDIC) finalist for *The National Training Achievement Award*. In his 25 years as a deputy chief, 15 were dedicated to "street duty" where he served as the Incident Commander in handling some of the City's most challenging fires, disasters, and other emergencies.

After attaining two associate degrees from The Community College of Philadelphia (CCP) in Public Management and Fire Administration, Gary earned a BS in Fire Science from The University of Maryland. He holds a Master's Degree from St. Joseph's University in Training and Organizational Development. Other noteworthy academic achievements include Executive Fire Officer certification from the National Fire Academy, completion of the Industrial Fire Protection Program at Texas A & M University, and a Certified Fire Protection Specialist status from the National Fire Protection Association.

In addition to having several articles published, Gary has earned CCP's prestigious *Judith Stark Creative Writing Award*. He has lectured on leadership, training, and other topics in numerous public and private sector organizations and has served as an adjunct instructor at The

AN INTROSPECTION

Community College of Philadelphia, Montgomery County Emergency Training Center, Neumann University, and St. Joseph's University. Additionally, Gary has enjoyed strong ties with his police "brothers/sisters in blue" by serving as an adjunct instructor in Alvernia University's Criminal Justice Administration Program and holding a seat on CCP's Justice Program Advisory Board.